MW00736751

MOUSTACHE PETE IS DEAD!

EVVIVA BAFFO PIETRO!
(LONG LIVE MOUSTACHE PETE!)

ITALIAN/AMERICAN ORAL TRADITION
PRESERVED IN PRINT

THE *FRA-NOI* COLUMNS 1985-1988

FRED L. GARDAPHÉ

BORDIGHERA

Library of Congress Cataloging-in-Publication Data

Gardaphé, Fred L.
    Moustache Pete is dead! : evviva Baffo Pietro! (long live Moustache
Pete!) : Italian/American oral tradition preserved in print ; the Fra
noi columns, 1985-1988 / Fred L. Gardaphé.
       p.   cm. -- (VIA folios ; 13)
    ISBN 1-884419-13-5 (alk. paper)
    1. Italian Americans--Social life and customs. I. Title. II. Series.
E184.I8G37   1997
973 '.0451—dc21   97-43451
                                         CIP

COVER ART: BOB CIMBALO

© 1997 by Fred L. Gardaphé

Printed in the United States.

Published by

BORDIGHERA INC.
WEST LAFAYETTE, IN

ISBN 1-884419-13-5

To Paolina Bianco Rotolo,

whose voice I could only imagine.

The Origins of Moustache Pete

A Preface

For nearly three years I provided the *Fra Noi* newspaper with a column entitled "Moustache Pete." Its origins are best explained through responses to readers' letters that came to the paper regarding the column. While there were many positive responses, the negative letters brought out a defense that I now, nearly ten years later, offer as a way of introducing this book.

The first, since it came from a public official, required my formal response as Arts & Culture editor; the second was Pete's own response to a letter.

August 14, 1986

Mr. Village President

Dear Mr. VP,

Your letter of August 7th has been referred to me for an appropriate response. I would like to thank you for taking the time to write to the *Fra Noi*. We appreciate your encouragement as well as your criticism.

As Arts Editor I have received many compliments and complaints concerning our Moustache Pete. I must admit I never thought it would stir up as much controversy as it has. As to your concerns, let me first say that if such a column appeared in anything other than an Italian American journal, the *Fra Noi* would certainly be concerned. However the column as it appears in the *Fra Noi* is not intended to be derogatory nor insulting. On the contrary, its intentions are humble and honest.

Let me give you some history as to its production. Six years ago I began recording oral histories of first generation Italian immigrants. During this time I became aware of how hard those people struggled to adapt to America. Very often, because of looks and language they were discriminated against. This treatment, however, did not stop them from telling the truth and living honest, exemplary lives. They were pioneers who gave their lives to make ours (the following generations') easier. During this time I was also reading the more than 100 oral histories gathered by the Italians in Chicago Project, directed by Dr. Dominic Candeloro, and writing a regular feature column for the *Fra Noi* called "Villa Profile," which consisted of interviewing residents of the Villa Scalabrini Home for the Aged.

Moustache Pete is based on an actual man, still alive today, who made me see that my past will always be a part of who I am and what I do. Most importantly, he helped me to understand why I was embarrassed when my grandparents spoke broken English, and helped me find the music in their speech.

He agreed to monthly visits to record his thoughts and experiences about life. His one request was that I not change the way he speaks. His comment was, "It's the truth I speak, not the way I speak, that must be understood. If I'm gonna speak to the people who read this paper, I want them to hear me just as I sound."

I've agreed to honor this simple request because soon Pete's generation will be gone. I believe that it's important for us not to deny their existence—broken English and all.

I'd be happy to discuss this further if you'd like. Thank you for your interest in this matter.

Sincerely yours,
Fred L. Gardaphe
Arts & Culture Editor

The following appeared in the February, 1986 "Moustache Pete" column:

When editor Fred firs' tell me he wan' me to talk to the people I was thinkin', What can I have to say? Who wanna lissen to an old timer like me?' But over the months I think I'm havin' a good time and at least I'm not hurtin' nobuddy. I say if they want to listen to a story or two I got plenty. Besides it's no more like in the old days, when everyone would sit around and talk. So when I'm talkin to you in the paper, is for me like the old days. I look forward to when Mr. Fred comes each month and writes down what I say.

I was so surprise las' month when Mr. Fred tell me I got some mail. I was thinkin' must be a bill collector or somet'in cause nowdays no good news come for me in the mail, nobuddy sen' me letters. If they got sommmatin to tell me they call up onna phone or see me in the park. Well I open up this letter and it says:

Dear Editor,
How can you fight defamation and discrimination in an article on page one and publish Moustache Pete in of all places on the Arts page. That column has got to go. It does nothing but remind us of what we've gotten away from. My family has worked hard to leave the past behind; we don't want to read that trash.

Well I'll be the firs' one to say that maybe my words aren't real art. They my life. But I tell Mr. Fred to put down jus' like I say or I say nothin'. Where they let me talk in the paper is they business. But I gotta say I seen worse art.

You know someatin I doan have no idea what is this guy talkin about "defamation"?

Was funny. I doan know what the word mean, so I ask Mr. Fred and he tell me it means 'attacking the good reputation of someone, or to slander or libel." Then I ask him what is "slander"? I was thinkin means "skinny" or someat'in like that. He tell me means to defamate someone in you speech. Then he tell me that libel is to do it in writing.

Was funny. I have been call many things in my life: dago, wop, guinea and greaseball, but no one ever call me defamation. Then I ask Mr. Fred what does this guy mean? And he tell me he thinks this guy means I ruin the good reputation of Italians. Now what do you think of that?

Then I ask Mr. Fred what should I do. He said that maybe I should write a letter back to this man. I say is a good idea. So here goes:

Dear Mr. that call me defamation,

Let me tell you what is goin on here. I was mindin my own business one day when Mr. Fred call me up and ask to interview me. Says for history. So I invite him over and we talk all day. He is a good man. He listen and ask good questions. Talkin is someathing I like to do.

A few months later Mr. Fred says how would I like to tell my stories to lots of people. I say, sure. Just tell them to come over. When he tell me is goan be thousands of people, I say 'scuse me Mr. Fred you craze. I can no fit thousands of people in my house. Then he splain that I tell my stories to him and he write them down. Then he put them in this paper.

Now I was thinkin. I never write nothing down. Is too much trouble. What happen if you change you mind about somethin? Is hard to erase somethin thousands of times. But he say we don't print nothin that will get us in trouble. We just goan tell the truth in some stories.

Well now Mr. who write me the letter, I think you got me in some trouble. But you can only get me for slander. I just say things. You have to blame the libel on Mr. Fred.

But you know, I think you, Mr. letterwriter, is the one who is libel me. You call me defamation and I'm no defamation. I am jus' who I am. If you no like what I say or how I say it, then doan read it. If you think I'm no good for the reputation of Italians in this country, then tell me Mister Big Words, who is?

Do I embareass you? Then I'm sorry. But you doan call me defamation less you got proof; that's what I learn in America. You can get in a lotta trouble for that.

When Mr. Fred read me your letter I say one thing, you sound good English. You doan know how hard I work jus' to speak as good as I do an that's not too bad. How good you speak Italian?

You gotta remember one thing Mistah. I'mma who you come from. You can be better than me only because someone like me go through a whole lotta trouble so that you can be born here. If you wanna forget is you business. I can no forget. Maybe when we die you can pretend we never were here, but what you goan do about our ghosts?

I remain,
Moustache Pete

"Moustache Pete" survived only three years. In August of 1988, a new editor took over the paper and Pete was the first thing to go. The editor thought it was derogatory trash.

ACKNOWLEDGMENTS

My greatest debt is owed to my grandparents, whose wisdom, no matter the language, has taught me how to respect my elders. They also taught me how to listen to and through someone's voice. Through their stories, advice and directions, they passed on to me an oral tradition that I have been able to preserve in print.

Father Armando Pierini, Father Lawrence Cozzi, publishers and Jim Ylisela, Jr., the editor of *Fra Noi* during these years, all gave me the opportunity and support to explore Italian American culture and to produce these and other writings. Finally, I thank Anthony Julian Tamburri and Paul Giordano of Bordighera, Inc. for seeing this book as a worthwhile project.

FRED L. GARDAPHE
Winter 1997

ONE — APRIL 1985

> "There are few serious studies of Italian Americans, particularly current ones. It is easy to see why this has left accounts of their past, their present and their future expressed almost exclusively in the dubious logic of stereotypes."
>
> Richard Gambino, *Blood of My Blood*

EDITOR'S NOTE:

Out of the shadows steps Moustache Pete. He is a short man, dark skinned, dark haired with nose that curls down to his bushy moustache. Moustache Pete is a *cantastoria*, in Italian that means "history singer;" he is what other cultures call a "griot." He remembers what we used to be. He carried with him "la via vecchia" to "la terra nuova." He remembers so that we may never forget. And every month from now on, he will have a chance to speak to you through Fred Gardaphe's transcriptions of his oral recordings.

I must say myself that is quite an introduction. I never go so much for the big words and the studies, but is not for me to say nothing. I'm just happy to be talking to you, and they tell me as long as I got something to say they gonna let me talk to you every month. Any way, is not right to talk without introducing yourself, so here I go.

My name is Moustache Pete. I was born in Italy. Where, you ask? To tell you the truth, I forget. Anyway, makes a no difference where one is born or where one a dies. What makes the difference in a life is no where, but how one lives. I was one of maybe 13 children and we had hard life.We have a saying that goes, "Chi sta a casa, sta secco, e chi esce s'ingrandisce." Oh forgive me, I forget, so many can no speak the old language, no more. Lemme see if I can translate for you: "He who stays home will shrink like a prune, but he who gets out will go full bloom." So long time ago I leave my family and for most my life I live in a place call Chicago. I leave Italy a long time ago an was crowd on a boat for ten maybe twelve days. When I see that statue of the lady America with a torch in her hand I was never so happy I think maybe she was la madonna.

I get offa Ellis Island in the night and when I come to the city Nuova York, I see they was torches onna street. Now I'mma think to my self, Pietro, cause that was my name before I become 'merican. What a wonderful country that can turn night into day. And I say Pietro, they say there's gold inna streets of La Merica. Can it be they burn torch lights so that people can mine the gold all night long? When I come, boy was I a greenhorn. I could no speak the language. I look for the street where the train is and every street was written Ave Fifth; Ave Seventh; St. Forty-Second; St. Market. I think to myself, 'am so lucky to come to a country where they welcome you to streets and name them after Saints and Holy people.

I come a to Chicago onna Erie Railway. Wasa not too bad a trip. A lil bumpy but what can you do, eh. Anyway I come to Polk Depot and where I get offa train. I didn't know where to go. I have address of a boarding house on a piece of paper, a few dollars stuck in my shoe and right away I get a lil hungry. So I look for something to eat. I see a man sell onna street fruit. So I point to a nice apple, show him a dollar that I have in my hand and he laughs and takes the money. I take out my knife to peel the apple and all offa sudden he stop laugh, give me all his money and raise his hands up, like he was afraid. Now I was maybe greenhorn, but I was a no stupid greenhorn. What kind country is this that pay you to buy? Would be wonderful if was true, but even no greenhorn like me believe this.

So while I was thinkin about all this come a copper and knock the apple an knife out my hand with stick and then knock me in the head. I ask why Mista Policeman hit me, and he say some-a-thing like, all you dagoes carry knives and make trouble. It make no difference because I no hear what he say then, for the ring in my ears. Anyway I get out of jail after a few days, cause the people I come to live with find me and everything get explain. I neva did get that knife back.

Firs' t'ing I do is to find a way to make my living. I'm tellin ya when I start to work diggin a ditch I wasa ready to go back to where I come from. I did work in my life that seven horses could not do. Now doan get me wrong. I don't mind digging, but in Italy I use to dig the land to plant live things: plants and flowers that some day grow to feed and make a man happy. What I wasa plantin wasa dead things: made of crushed stone and dirt. Was no good way to keep a man like me happy, but, eh what was I goan do? Felt like I was a slave makin pyramids or somethin. But lot of us had to do things we didn't like just to survive, right?

Today, some-a people don't think unions is good. Oh how we fight for the unions. Was a good idea those unions, keep us from becomin slaves. Why I remember one day when we was a work inna ditch. The foreman call us all together and tell us they wasa goan cut our wages in half. Said it was a hard time for everbody. So my friend Pasquale, he was a funny man. A honest and tough man. He tell me, hey Pete, put your chisel onna my shovel, right about there. He was workin longer than me so I do what he say. I put the chisel at the top of his shovel right about half way. Then with a sledge hammer in one hand he pound on that chisel and cut the shovel in half. The bossman come up to him and say, "Pasquale, what you think you do?" Ole Pasquale say, "Mistah boss man, iffa you cut my wages in 'alf, I cutta the shovel in 'alf." Now there was a real Italian. When the ground she froze I tell you was rough for a boy like me, who use to the mild weather of Bell'Italia. We could no more dig and I was again look for work.

For a while I work inna factory, but then the Depression come and take away all my work. Everyone was walkin around like an old widow in black. But me, I was no worry. "Il contadino ha le scarpe rozze e il cervello fino": you know what mean? It means the peasant has rough shoes, but a sharp brain. I t'ink is not so bad to be poor, so long as you eat. "Poche ricchezzi pochi pensieri": Few riches, few worries. I maybe not have much money, but I have much happiness in them days. I find money in what people throw way. I was for a while goin down the street and picking up the old rags and iron that I could find. I would make a little money sellin them and all day long I would hear from the people. There goes the wop and you know what I tell them, of course after I learn a little how to talk 'merican. I say: "I'm a dago; you the wop. I eat spaghetti; you eat slop." Yeah, they use to call me all kinda names: Dago, wop, guinea, greaseball, meatball, spaghetti bender. Wasa hard thing to listen to those names, why sometime I get mad and punch, but mostly I just smile and pretend I don't hear nothing. I tell you something too, if you work inna dirt the grease anna mud, you be a greasyball too.

Two — May, 1985

You know, I never understan too much the artists. I use to think they was just a bunch of lazaroni, afraid to do real work. I think maybe they jus' wan dream and make things you can no eat. But I wasa wrong. A good artist can make you see someathing you never see before. Even if you was staring at it all day long. I doan know much about the thinking of art, but I know when I likea somethin it make me feel good. An' that's good enough for me.

This month the editor, he aska me, Pete, whattya got to say a'bout writing. I say is ok. I mean, I never write a book or nothin. If a man make me think 'bout somethin more than once, he is good. If he remind me of something I forget, he's good too. But if he tell me somethin I never forget, then he is great, then he is an artist with words. An if I doan forget, then I doan have to write.

That's what I like about writing. But I doan know so many writers. Oh you got Dante and all the others, but when we come over here we didn't know the language to speak and so how we goan write? I know one man who coulda been a great writer, but he work inna ditch all his life. He build the street that his gran kids now drive big fancy cars over. He tell so many stories. He was so good to tell the story that I doan mind to hear the same story twice in a row. That's how good he was.

I ask him, I say, "Luigi, where you get all these stories?" cause every day he tella me a new one. He says to me, "Pete, stories come from ever'w'ere. For a good story you have to listen."

I say, "But Luigi, I listen to all you stories and when I tell them to other people is never the same. I never get right like you. He tells me, "Pete to listen to someone else is ok, but you also gotta listen inside the story. You gotta listen to what the story is sayin right when you tellin it." Now that make me scratch my head, because I never before thought to listen to a story that I was tellin. I try, but I still doan getta right. So I say to Luigi, "Must be a gift you have. Maybe if you write you down all you stories, into a book, maybe then I would get them right." He tell me,"I think is for me to live the book, maybe to tella story to my children an' let them write it down. But I never tell the story the same way, so how can I decide how to write down. One day maybe I write it one way, the next day maybe another. Besides how I'm goan learn to write a language I can hardly speak. No, I can never do somethin like write a book. I come to this country to make a good life so that maybe my children can work the art. You can no make art when the family have always the empty stomach. No?"

I guess he'sa right, No? And for that I give him respect. And since I meet him I have more respect for writers. "Rispetto," you remember what is rispetto? I come here an work all my life for rispetto. Was a hard job when you no speak the language and you wan respect. My boys fight inna all the wars, some they even die for this country. That is a way to earn respect, but is too late to respect a man when he's dead. To become educate and to make good things, like books and motion picks and theater and art and food; to do a good job and blame no one but youself if you make a mistake, that is the way to respect. An never do nothin that will make you lose respect for youself. A man can lose respect for others and live, but when he lose respect for himself, he dies. To earn respect you have to live a good life. "Chi rispetta rispettato sarà." He who respects others will be respected. So I learn to respect people who make good art. They take a lot of time to do they work. Good things take good time.

Luigi tell me once that ever man have wonnerful stories to tell. Some tell only to themselves. And is good enough for them. Some tell to the family and some tell to the whole world. What is the difference as long as they get told, right?" But I say, "What if no one remembers the story?" And you know what he tell me? He say, "If no one remembers then was only two problems could be: was a bad story in the begin or was bad listener." That Luigi, he always make me think.

Back in the old country an' even in the old neighborhood, we use to get together an talk. In the piazza, outside the church, on the streets in front of our houses, even in the store. Could take two hours to buy a loaf of bread once you start talkin, and more if wasa good story to hear. But today everbody inna rush. People doan take the time to talk no more, to tell the stories. People talk more on machines then they do in person. When is the last time you heard a good story on a telephone? Maybe is why people complain about how the good things is life are hard to find. Fasta cars, fasta food, what do they bring you but accidents and acida. I think people have forgot how to wait. Back in the old country was no problem to wait for things. Waiting give you time to think. When you rush you never get someathing good. "Presto maturo, presto marcio": Quick to ripe is quick to rot.

You know writers are just people who take they time to talk to you and, if you think, then maybe you read some more, eh? A good writer can slow ever'ting down, can make some things live forever, can make you listen, no?

THREE — JUNE, 1985

I tell you, today things look pretty good. I never think I see the day when Italian people have it so good. You know something. I tell you a little secret; but doan tell nobuddy. We was a not always white.

Maybe you too young to remember but long time ago, I think was in New Orleans, they lynch thirteen paesani and some places when they have problem they pick on the Italians, like wid Sacco an' Vanzetti. Hey, look at me. When I get a few days of sun on my skin, you know, the look that everyone with lots of money spend months in foreign places to get, I don't look like I'mma white. And back in the old days you can bet nobody take me for white. "La persona che nasce pera non puo essere pesca": the person who is born a pear can no be a peach.

People use to laugh at me when I talk, but I tell you was no jokes what I was tellin. Was the way I speak. I see on televish once a man who dress like a priest, was try to be Mr. Funny Man. Call himself Guido Sarducci. He talk likea me. Now, I talk like this cause I nev had the school. Because I talk like this I can no get just any job I want. Keep me from makin money and this 'lazarone' make a fortune doin what cost me maybe a fortune. Is a funny life, no?

My sons and daughters they no speak like me. Now I hear is ok speak two languages, is even good to be what they call bi-lingual, but when I raise my kids I make sure they learn English, cause Italian was doin them no good in this new country. Sometimes I'm sorry I did that, cause there's somethings in the old language that they can no understand and they is no words in this new language to express them.

Like 'ben educato.' It don't mean the education you get from the state in schools. It means what you learn about life.

Anyway, I educate them and then put them to work. Have to. How else they goan learn to enjoy life if they no learn to work. So what do they do? They send their kids off to fancy school. To get 'merican educated. They wear nice clothes ever day. They graduate in fancy ceremonies and go offa to college to forget everting they was taught in the house. We no need school in the old country so much because they was lessons ever day inna house. How to take care of house for the girls and how to take care of outside the house for the boys. Is ok, no?

Take look at my grandkids now. They marry and you think you see kids in nine months like you used to. No! Now I think it takes nine years to make one kid. Then if I'm lucky they make one more. Is not even enough to name the relatives after. But is ok. Is what I come to America for no? To do what I can to make good life. I guess the reason I see so much trouble cause to make a garden you gotta start in the dirt. You take a seed, like me, you plant in the soil and soon if is taken care of it grows through the rocks, it makes roots, it shoots up and reaches for the sun. The rain come with the storm and you grow and then if you have good luck and good times, then you have something good to harvest.

Nowadays is ok to cross breed, sometime it makes for a better, stronger plant, any one who works with the land knows this. Now in my time you never see so much cross breed; the Irish stay with the Irish; the Polish stay with the Polish; and the Italian with the Italian; I tell you one think, you wanna know something? Is no plants like the plants in bell'Italia. I tell you they doan use no chemicals back where I come from. Well, I guess they startin to since they import all the scientists from the USA. But when I taste a fruit or a plant from Italy, I know just from the taste that is givin me life.

So what is Old Pete doin here? I look around today and see there's no more like me around. I wonder where they all go. Maybe I fine them all in a church or inna churchyard. Who knows? But I come around to see how my people is doin. And you know, is hard to tell my people anymore. If they no wear t-shirts and buttons like that say "Kiss me I'm Italian," I tell you, many times I mistake others for my people.

Imma told you can tell the people by the art. So I look everywhere today. I look inna theatre and who do you think I see? Is like a wax museum. They so polished, look Italian but they don't act Italian. They got more gold on they necks than Cleopatra. And I hear that some of these crazy films are made by Italian people. I'mma tell you isa no way they would make Italians into these stupid people if they knew what Italians did for this country.

I see in the movies that so many Italians shoot guns. Now don't think that I doan know about the gangsters. Why some of every group got gangsters, but if you look inna motion picts, you think they was all Italian. To be godfather in my day was an honor. Now is to be a gangster. You doan know what a gangster is! A gangaster is a cheap punk who knows you can make a lot more money scaring people than you can selling. Where I come from was the weak and sick who try to be gangster. Why they get so much attention I never understand.

Proud to be Italian. But what is to be proud? Proud yes, to work and build a country that wants freedom, that even fights for freedom. But remember, pride goes before a fall. So what does proud to be Italian mean? I doan know. I know I wasa proud to be 'merican and want to forget sometimes I was Italian. So many Italians I know change they name.

Was a hard job to become 'merican. Had to learn the ways and the language and the test for be a citizen. Had to give up many of the old ways, but never the old values. I neva cheat to get ahead; I try to help people when I can; I respect them and they respect me. I try to make friends with people because is nice to have friends all over the place. It makes the big world a little smaller a little less strange when you make another friend.

I had friends all over Chicago: in places call the Patch, over 4th and Sherman; the Dive, over by 12th St. bridge; Little Hell, was over by Chicago Avenue; Tenderloin, over at 22nd an Clark St.; the Pepper Patch, inna Melrosa Park; Hungry Hill, inna Chicago Heights; the Valley, inna Roseland-Pullman; Taylor Street an Terra Cotta an 24th and Oakley. Today I can no find the places I used to go. I doan see my friends sit outside playin bocce, morra, briscola an lickin a lemonade or talkin to each other. What they do nowadays, I no know.

When I come to Chicago, was no more than a few thousand of us and today I count more than 500 thousands. Is no place no more like Little Italy, today is little pieces of Italy scatter all across the city like dandelion seeds in the winds. So what happen to the things we brought over from Italy with us? We didn't bring over Michaelangelo, Da Vinci, or Dante, they was already here when we got here. But we come over many artists, poets, singers.

Now me I nev been to Rome, Florence or Venice, but you would think that everthing Italian in this country come from the North. Is funny that no matter where you go is always fighting between the north and the south. Why long before I come to this country was fight right here between the north an south.

What we bring to this country is honest people who are not afraid to work for what they want. I didn't come here to escape something I came to have just opportunity to do with my life what I want.

When you think about it, is too much water in this world. There's a water inna drink, inna food, inna brain. Pretty soon one hundred percent of everything will be water, like was in the Noah story. Everbuddy on a big boat inna big water. There needs to be more vino in this country. Vino e vinegar: vino for to calm a man an vinegar for to put some fire in him. I know a man who live to be one hundred. Every morning he drink a shot of vinegar, he say to get his heart going and every night he drink vino, he say to help him slow down a little bit. Think about it. I do ever'day. See you nex' month.

FOUR — JULY, 1985

Is that time time of the year again for Le Feste della Madonna ed i Santi. Is a special season for an old timer like me because the feste bring me back in time. I feel young again when I hear la banda an the firecracks. Somea way le feste are like fountains of youth.

You wanna know why I like all the Feste? An whether you see me there or no, I'mma always there. I can tell you I never miss one. I like them cause I get to see all my old friends and they families. The days of the feste are hot but like we say, "Amici e maccheroni, se non sono caldi, non sono buoni." That means friends are like macaroni if they not warm they no good. An that's what the feste are for: to bring together all you friends. But I gotta tell you is no more like the old days. These days the feste get more an more 'merican. You know what I mean?

No doan get me wrong. I doan say they no good. For how can you come to a new country an not become part of it. I mean I think the feste are losing some things.

Not too many people remember no more why they is the feste. Back in the old country they was a time to stop work and to celebrate all the good things we get from God. Like here in La Merica we have the Thanksgiving. That is what the feste are like. In Italia they was the feste in the spring to celebrate planting, in the fall to celebrate the harvest and on special days of the saints to celebrate the help we get from God through them. Wasa time to rest from work.

In those days was no stoppin the work like we can do here in America, every few days. You can no tell the crops to take a day or two off or the weeds to slow down a little bit. You can no tell the cow and the sheep and the goats to take care of them selves while you rest. I can remember when I was a boy we use to take the animals with us to the feste. Some we bring to kill and cook. Then everbody join together like we was one big family and share the food.

When I come to this country we make the feasts because it make us to remember "bell'Italia." Wasa a time for all us Italians to get together and celebrate our way of life. We use to take the horses or trucks or trolleys from the city to the country. Wasa a long trip and we use to bring the homemade food to have for picnic. Was a big thing in those days to travel so far, take hours then what takes minutes today. Makes me wonder what people do with alla time they have these days.

These days you go to the feste and can buy food that is ready to eat. Do old Pete a favor. When you eat the sausage sandwich I want you to think of all the work we use to do to raise those animals, the ones we had to kill to help us live. Wasa hard work, dirty work that we no more have to do. Now we got machines to do it. But was not always like this.

In the old days was like we were people in the bible times, making sacrifice of the animals. A knife to the throat of a goat, a hatchet to the chicken head was what you do if you gonna eat. Now these things are done far away and brought to us covered in plastic. If you ask me the taste is no the same, but "Come ci fa?" Whatta you gonna do? Is progress they say. No?

Is a whole new world we come to when we leave Italia. We try to make some things like they was, but is still some thing different. Now don't get me wrong. I doan complain about 'merica. I just some time miss the old country and the way we use to do things.

You see those fancy lights at the feste? Not too long ago we didn't have the 'lectric lights. Was just candles we use to light up the night. Those candles was made by the young girls and they mothers an aunts. Imma told that before they was candles people use to light torches and carry them in the procession. Was a way to show rispetto to the Madonna and to the Saints like San Gennaro, San Rocco, an all the rest.

You know the feste to us Italians is like Christmas an New Years all over again. We celebrate our religion an we celebrate our lives. The feste are a way to mark time, a way to look back but also to look ahead. So when you go to the feste this year, remember that maybe was different in the old days, but they still are for the same old things: God, our families an our way to live. If you remember these things then you make an old man like me pretty happy.

I think maybe I'm just like the old saying, "Il giovane vuole cambiare il mondo. Il vecchio vuole cambiare il giovane." You know what means? It means the young boy wanna change the world and the old man, he wanna change the young boy. Come ci fa?

FIVE — AUGUST, 1985

"Le cose vanno meglio nel racconto." This an olda saying that mean things always go better in the telling. An that's the way it goes. I tell you my whole life goes on and someatime I doan know what happen until after while when I think about it some. Is the same with you?

When I looka back an remember someating it neva seem bad as it was. Things that was terrible once upon a time doan seem so bad when you look back. Maybe is because when you live a while you see that evert'ing mixes up in life.

Likea time I come 'ere onna boat. Was a terrible times. People was gettin sick. We didn't t'ink we was goan make it. Was too crowd you know. People was leanin over the rail and cursin' the sea. Some paesani even die right there inna belly of the boat, men, women, children an even li'l bambini, had to bury them inna sea to keep from disease. Unbelievable. Eh?

Was terrible when it happen, but years later it doan seem so bad. I mean, maybe I doan remember so good, or maybe I remember the good more than the bad, but one thing I never forget, was when we get into La 'merican harbor we see this biga statue. People was gettin' all excited, everbody wasa cryin and singin' "Ave Maria, Stella del Mare," "Hail Mary Star of the Sea." Is funny now to think that back then we believe was a big statue of La Madonna there in the water when really was Statue of Liberty.

All these people who was cursin an complainin an cryin onna boat, all of a sudden is like they was havin a party. An later, when someone ask them what was like onna boat, they say was no so bad. What you think of that? I guess is like the old saying, "Cambia il pane per la pietra," When you get stones change them into bread.

Six — September, 1985

When I wasa grow up in Italy I wen' a school for maybe two days. School in my land start right when was harvest time. The first day of school, boy I was so happy to think I would get out of work, but I shoulda know better. Right when we get to the story about the Romans, my father come an knock down the door. He say he need me in the fields. So he pull me right out of the school. The other day was so cold in the school that everbuddy sit on they hands and listen to the teach until they fall sleep. That was my time in school.

You see back in the old country nobuddy need school. An they was no girls in our school back then. The ladies use to think that if you teach your daughter to read and write that she goan write love letters to some stranger. Wasn't too many boys in our school either. What could school teach that the old timer couldn't tell us. Was no school to tell us how to milk a goat or bake bread or how to make the garden grow. You wan learn how to do somethin you go to someone who does it and work with them. That's how you learn back then.

But when we come to La Merica was a different story. All of sudden was so important to go to school. I never did go to school, but cause I didn't wanna be un-LaMerican I send my kids to school. I tell you I doan think it did my kids any good. Oh, doan get me wrong, they got the good educaysh. Some got degrees in medicine an' law an some even become the teach. But you know somethin, I wonder joosta how smart they are iffa they gotta watch televish to find out if goan rain or snow.

One time my boy he call me up and say pop, better put you storm windows up, soon is gonna snow. I tell him he's crazy. I can smell when a snow is commin and is no where near. Is gonna be one more warm stretch I tell him. But you think he listen to me? No. So when the Indian summer come along he can't breed in his house cause he got it already all locked up for winter. That's what his fancy educaysh got him, a stuffy house.

I tell you I think the more people go to school the dumber they get. They get so they can no depend on they own common sense no more. They buy junk inna store, stead of raisin' they own food inna garden; why pay good money for somethin you can have for a little hard work and some grace of God. Trouble with this country is too much educaysh. Why even got it on the televish. They's people who talk to the televish and never to they family. The kids move far away from they family to find a better life an' they talk family bizness onna phone stead of face to face.

Now you tell me, "Eh Pete, that's what you did. You leave Italy to come here." But I tell you when I leave Italy was because they was no chance to make a good life there. But here, in La Merica you can make a good life right next door to you family, just as good as goin thousand miles away. I break up my family in Italy so that I can make it better one day for my own family. But now my family is spread out all round this big country.

I doan know what is gonna happen to all those people with book smarts. I think sometimes they gotta read so much because they forget how to read life with they own eyes and ears. They get so they always need advice from some expert before they can do something simple. What's wrong with just talkin, talkin and listenin' that was what educaysh in my day. My father talk and I listen. But come ci fa? What you goan do? Is a whole new world since they drop the bomb, eh?

SEVEN — OCTOBER, 1985

"Il lavoro racconta la storia dell'umanita." Work tells the story of humanity. That's what the old timers used to say. That mean you can tell a lot about a people by the work they do. When we come to this country we was look for work all-a time. I'mma tell you that we would do anything to find a way to live. Some a guys even take to playin the hurdy-gurdy an make dance with the monkey jus to get a few pennies. Like a street performer today.

Back in bell'Italia we work an get paid by the food we grow. In America, we work an have to buy the food with the little money we make. We went from work for food to work for money. I doan know which was worse.

When we get over to La Merica they was just freein' the slaves, but you couldn't fool us. We knew that we had become the new slaves. Some of my paesani signed away the best years of they life for a chance to come over to the freedom and work that America was promising. And when we get over here, all we find is a lot of work for a little money.

Becase we doan know the language we had to trust our paesano, the 'padrone,' the man who meet us at the boats and promise us work and shelter. I can't tell you how many times he take our money and give us nothin but problems. But we live through all that and made it better for our kids. We work hard and some of us even die to build strong unions that help us keep our dignity and free us from being slaves. I was talkin to a buddy of mine the other day an he was tellin me a story that says a lot about what's happened to us Italo Americani.

He tell me, "You know Pete, I work a job like a slave until the union was formed. If it wasn't for that union I woulda never been able to have my nice house, send my kids to schools, take a vacation or live nice in retirement, like I do. Now my son tells me that a friend of his is workin to break that union. Yeah, they both went to the same law school. Now my son he works for the government and this friend of his for some big downtown law firm. That kid's grandfather was one of the leaders of that union back when I work in it. And now that kid is workin to destroy everything his grandfather built. I doan understand it."

That's a something that I can un'erstan'. You see, that poor kid was pushed to become 'merican', you know, go to college, become a lawyer, get a good job; he didn't take the time to learn what life was like for his grandpa. He's can say he's only doin his job and really believe he's doing right. He never grow up needin what the union helped his grandpa get. And so he doesn't even know what he's doin.

I think no matter how good we have it, we should raise our kids with some sense of hard work an with a taste of what is like to work with they hands. If we don't then they will never appreciate life. If they know what is like to have blisters on they hands and feet, maybe then they won't be afraid the help people whose hands are covered with calouses.

We gotta make sure that the way we work and the way we live says good things about our humanity. If work tells the story of our people, then somebuddy better make sure that the story that is told is worth listening to.

EIGHT — NOVEMBER, 1985

When I wasa grow up was no thing likea radio or televish. We fine out about what happens from someabuddy who been there or someabuddy who hear from someabuddy else.

We no have what you call mass media, we have media mass. After church alla people would stand outside church an tell ever one what was go on. If we wanna fine out about sometin we go to the piazza. Was our version of the evenin news. You walk from the group of old men to learn history, to the young men to learn news and to the youngest to learn gossip. We had equal opportunity too. The women can tell the news just as good as a man. An some a them was even better reporters than the men.

I never forget the time somebuddy say to me, "Pete did you hear that so and sos mamma die. I cross myself and say, "No kiddin. I'm gonna stop by an see the family." When I get to the house I shoulda known somethin was wrong cause there was no sign on the door. I feel bad, that maybe they no have enough money to buy a ribbon or a wreath. So I go to the shop and pick up some black ribbon. Now this lady was a good friend of my mamma's so I take out a few extra lira and buy a little wreath. I go back to the house and am happy to see they is still no wreath. They will appreciate my gift.

I knock on the door and she open slow. I take off my hat, bow my head, and while holdin the ribbons and the wreath out, I say, "I give you my sympathy on the death of..." Then I look up. The wreath fall from my hands. My mouth open and nothing more come out. I turn white an start to shake. There standin at the door was the lady who die. Was unbelievable. For the first time in my life I see a smilin ghost. Seem like a day pass before I could hear what the lady was sayin.

She say, "Oh hello Pete. What's wrong wid you. You look like you seen a ghost." Then she laugh like a crazy woman. I was scared. I neva hear a ghost talk or laugh. I was goan run away. Then she grab me. I close my eyes and pray to God. When I open my eyes she is laughin. She say, "So you heard I was dead too. Is not me that die, is la signora so an so. But was nice of you to think of me. Next time check out you source." Then she take the wreath and hit me on the head with it.

I tell that story cause that is what I think of all this mass media. Is just a fancier an faster way to get gossip around. Maybe a better name is mess media, cause all it do is show what a big mess we get into when we stick our nose in other people's business.

Who wanna see how the world suffer? What good does it do a man to see someone starvin? When I see that stuff I wanna reach into the crazy tube and hand them some money, or pat them on the back. But I no can do that. So, come ci fa? What you goan do?

•

NINE — DECEMBER, 1985

If I live to be one hundred I will never unnerstan what happen to Christmas. Whenna I was a boy I never dream that Christmas could be like today. I mean, was a good time if we had a few cookies. We always eat good, specially on Christmas, but we never worry so much for what to buy this person or that. Everbody have nothin so no buddy gets a gift. Christmas wasa time when ever buddy get together and enjoy the company. Wasa story my pappa use to tell us on Christmas and now I'm gonna give to you.

Once 'pon time they was a poor farmer. His wife she die young and leave him all alone to take care of the family. This man had so many kids no matter how hard he work, he never could feed them all. Could only feed them a few at a time. You know, one day he feed some, the next day a few more and so on, so that in one week ever buddy eat once.

One year his land stop growin food and so no buddy eat. On Christmas Eve the poor farmer was sittin outside his little hut cryin. "Oh God, if you doan help us we all goan die from no eat."

A man come by and see him and say, "Hey man, what's you problem?" The poor farmer look up with tears in his eyes and say, "Mister, my family goan die from hunger. My land is no good no more and I can no find work for to feed my kids." The man say to the farmer, "Don't cry. If you wan work, I give you work. I got some woods over there an I want to chop down allah trees and plant crops. If you like you can do it and I will pay you good. But you got to have it all finish tomorrow."

The farmer thank the man but shake his head, "Tomorrow is Christmas, the holiest day of the year. I can no work. If you let me I will do the job the next day." The man shake his head and say, "Well I guess you not so bad off. I'll see you." And he start to walk away.

Just then the kids, who hadn't eat for three days cry out for food. The farmer look at them, then run after the man. "Mister, come back. I will do your work." The man say, "Ok. You do the work and tomorrow I will come by and pay you."

The next morning the farmer wake up and say his prayers. He ask God to forgive him for workin on Jesus birthday. Then he go to work and by sundown he clear the whole field. He wait and wait for the man to come an pay, but the man never come. He was sitin on the ground and cryin, "Look at what I do. I work on the holiest day of the year, joosta so my kids can eat and now I'm a big fool."

Just then another man passed by and stopped. "What's you problem Mr. Farmer?" The farmer told the man the story and the man said. "But why you work on Christmas? You should stay home with you family."

The farmer say, "But my kids they were dying of hunger. What I'm suppose to do, eh?"

The man say, "If you are sorry for what you do, I will help you. Go home and you will find your pay. But never work again on Christmas." Then the man walk away. When the farmer get home he find his kids sitting by the table eating bread. He join them and for the first time in years they all eat together. They was happy even if was only bread they was eatin. The next year the same thing happen. The farmer had no work and on Christmas Eve he was praying to God for help. A man come by and tell him he can work, but has to be on Christmas. The farmer say no way. But when he hear his kids cry from hunger he break down and say ok.

On Christmas day he wake up early, say his prayers and then go off to work. When was done he wait and wait but no one come to pay him. He start crying and askin God to forgive him. Then another man come by and ask what is the problem. The farmer explain and the man say," But why you work on Christmas?" The farmer say was no choice. The man say, since was Christmas that he would help him out. He say, "Go home and you will find some pay."

The farmer go home an find his kids eatin bread at the table. Next Christmas Eve the very same thing happen, but this time when a man come by and offer him a job the farmer tell him forget about it. That night the farmer and his kids all go to bed hungry. When they wake up they was surprise to see a table filled with food. They say thanks to God and then they eat. And since then they live happily ever after. I hope you doan have to work on Christmas an I hope you have a very nice holiday. Buon Natale.

TEN — JANUARY, 1986

When I firs' come to La Merica I could no believe this winter. Oh, in Italy wasa cold, but not so cold that I couldn't work. An' the only snow was up inna mountains. But La Merica was different. Worse time was in Janwary. Wasa no so bad in December. Even when got cold, the ground was a still soft to dig. I remember I work like the devil in November and December. For the deeper you dig today, the easier it was the next day. I was happy to dig the deepholes. Cause once you get deep enough to hide you head, you no have to worry for the wind. But by Janwary, forget it. The ground was so hard, was like marble.

Winter wasa sad time for me. The sun hide away and instead of the rain like in Italy, we getta snow. I could smell the snow comin. Was like fresh fish. An when the snow start to fall it poke my neck like was a cold, wet finger.

I was afraid for the snow. Cause I know was goan take away my work. It would come someatime in big pieces that fall from the sky like some a one was throwin down lace curtains. An it wouldn't stop until the sun was all coverup.

When I was a young boy I never like the winter. It take away all the color, turn everthin into black and white and grey. Oh they was some days when the sun, she sneak a look at the world, and show us some pretty light, make the snow so bright you can't look at it straight in the eyes, but most of all the sun stay away and the world stay like an old photograph.

Worse of all was: "Viene inverno, va via lavoro,": when winter come, the job she go. That's how was for us greenhorns. I tell you I doan know why I stay around

Chicago inna winter. Musta been craze. Was no work in the early days, when I no speak English too good.

"Senza lavoro, senza vestito," to be without work is to be without clothes. That is what we use to say. There is no dignity in a naked man. An a man without a job is like a naked man. If I woulda had a good educaysh, maybe I could get a job inside. But no one help me out. I feel terrible. Here I was, a boy who has left his family and home and his warm sunny land to cross an ocean for work. Ever'tin' die inna winter.

So like a man who is naked will grab anythin to cover himself, I took whatever job I could fine. The winter could stop the digging for the job, for the people alive, but it couldn't stop for the dead. So every day when they was no workin in the streets, I would wake up and go down to the grave yard. I can tell you now. Every day I hope that someone die, jus so I could have a job to dig the grave. Is terrible now when I think back, but when you live for to work, you do anythin to keep from dyin without work.

Now you might say, Pete, why you tell us such a sad story? I gotta say I doan really know. But I just say it. I think is really a happy story hidin' in this.

These days, when I doan work so much I tell you I'm getting to like this winter. Is more quiet. Is more peaceful. Is no so much rush rush. Is easy to listen to you thoughts.

People doan seem so craze. They stay inna home more. I like to take a walk downa street, inna woods and even in the old grave yard where I use to dig. These days I see a whole different person in winter, one who is now my good friend.

ELEVEN — APRIL, 1986

I'ma always talk to you bout the past. Like was some history profess or someat'ing like that, but I tell you I'ma joosta man who remembers things. I hear that if you always tell the truth you never have to remember things. Seems like today is so much to know that they have to give numbers to what we do. Now I can remember good times and bad times. I can remember a man's face or a when some buddy do someat'ing nice. But when comes to numbers I have trouble.

I doan know for you, but for me to remember numbers don't get any easier when you get old. Anyway this month I was thinkin what to say and all of a sudden it hit me. Numbers. I have so many numbers in my life is no wonder they come up with computer. Soshsecurity, telephone, address, pension, identificaysh, is enough to drive an old timer like me craze. Is easy to get in big trouble if you doan keep track of all you numbers. If you lose you number you don't get anywhere.

I was in a bakery the other day, joosta for to buy some little treat. I was wait for someone to take my order. Now I doan like to stand around like somea big jamocha with nothin to do, so I start to talk to the lady at the counter. Well then this man who was a waitin says to me, "Wait till she call you number; then you can talk all you want." Now what do you think of that? Can't a man be friendly and make a little talk without having a number. Wasn't like this in the old days.

They tell me we got so many numbers because that's progress. But when evertin becomes a science I think maybe we got too much progress. Seems evertin has numbers. Prett soon maybe we goan lose names and take on numbers. What you wann be called? Joe or 1731, Julie or 1219.

Now some numbers we gotta have, but I think we have too many. Who cares if temperature is 42 degrees or 44 degrees, to me is no difference: hot is hot, cold is cold and in between is nice. And the same for times: who cares if is 4:32 or 4:33. You wait for somebuddy or they wait for you.

Numbers make you think you are exact and when you t'ink you exact that's when you getta trouble. People trust numbers someatime more than feelings. Like when a doctor check me up. He say, "Pete, how you feel." I say I'mma feel prett good. Then he stick a thermometer in my mouth. When is ready he take it out and read the number. He says, "You not feelin so good; you gotta high temperature." I say what does that stick know; it's only been in me for a few minutes. I'm know how I feel all my life. Then he say, "This thing doan lie; you better take it easy for a while." Now I doan know for you, but I doan need no number to tell me how good or how bad I feel. When I hear that from the doctor I say goodbye.

No doan take me wrong. I doan say to get rid of numbers. They good for someat'ings. I'mma joosta say that behind the number is someat'ing human, someat'ing real and if you forget about that maybe you goan someday hurt somebuddy.

TWELVE — MAY, 1986

"La mamma è l'anima, chi la perde non la guadagna." You know what that mean? It say, you mother and you soul, once you lose them you never get back.

My mother she die a long, long time ago, but I never forget her. She was one tough lady. I tell you she raised ten of us kids. And she did everything. They was no school in my days, and she was our teach. We were more afraid of her than any policeman. Joosta the way she look you in the eyes was enough to make you feel like you in jail.

In La Merica they is many stores. To us, my mamma was every store: she was a grocer with her garden, she was a restaurant with her cooking, she was a tailor, with her sewing. If was something she couldn't do, then we didn't need it.

When we have a problem, she tell us to take care of it ourself. Now you might think that maybe she was a littlebit laze, but you gotta know that with ten boys and girls, if we don't learn how to do things for ourself when we young, then we gotta learn it when we're older. Besides she got her hands full of things all the time.

My mamma never waste a thing. She use everything over and over. She use to tell us, 'When someatin stops being good for what it was made for, don't throw it away; use you mind to find some other way to use it." Like with our body heat.

I can remember when she wake us up early in the morning. She was already up for hours mixing up the goods for bread. She would shoo us out of the bed and then put the dough right in where we were sleeping, then she cover it with our sheets. She would use the warm bed we make for to help the bread dough rise. Was a pretty sharp lady, no?

That's what a mamma can do. She can find good in the bad, clean in the dirt, sun inna rain. And no matter what life bring to her she give back something better.

Like the time was a terrible frosty snow in our town. It come too early one year, before we can take the grapes and the olives off the branches. It ruin everting and we thought was the end of the world.

My mother go outside and pick up the snow, she mix in some fruit and we have a good treat. It didn't bring the crops back, but it kept our spirits from freezing up. She was like that.

She never say, "Come ci fa?" "What we goan do?" She always say, "Lo facciamo," "We goan do." And that was it. My father used to say that if she was a man, she would makea good general, cause she never accept defeat.

The last time I saw my mamma was my last day was in the old country. She knew she would never see me again, but she never let me see her cry about it. I thought I was commin here joosta for to make some money and then go back, but America wouldn't let go of me. That day I was walkin away from the house and when I get to the top of the hill I turn around to see her one more time.

I was thinkin maybe she wasa still lookin for me, but she wasn't; her back was bend to the ground, pulling up cicoria for dinner. That's how I remember her, turning away from someatin sad toward someatin that needed to be done.

So you see, I may have lost my mamma, but because of her, I never lose my soul. Happy Mother's day to all you wonderful mothers.

THIRTEEN — JUNE, 1986

"Il padre 'campa' dieci figli,
e dieci figli non possono
'campare' il padre."

You know this old saying? A pappa can keep ten kids alive,
but ten kids can no keep one pappa alive. I doan know who
think of it, must be somebuddy who knew my Pappa. When
wasa boy, I tell you I never see anyone work likea my
Pappa. He work so hard it scare me. They wasa nothin he
could no do.

He get up inna mornin and after a little coffee an bread
he go into the field and work. He take a little break for
lunch and then he work again, diggin, plantin, weeding and
pickin until wasa too dark to see you own han's. Then he
come home eat, sleep and do it all again the next day. As
soon as we could walk we wasa workin right by his a side.
Was no such think as play when I wasa boy. Everbuddy, my
four brothers an I work right with him. We start together at
one end of a field. The boys onna one side Pappa on the
other. We work face to face an move sideaways, like we
wasa crabs or someatin. I'm tellin you no matter how hard
we work, Pappa would soon leave us far behind. Like a
machine he work.

He wasa what we call "un uomo furioso" a furious man. I
grew up all my life afraid of him. Even I was afraid when he
was sleepin. He would sleep furious. We could no make a
soun' when he sleep because we wasa ten kids all livin inna a
small house. One bigga room downasteers an one bigga
room upasteers. One atime was everone sleep. My brother
wake up onna night mare an wasa actin like a craze boy. He

holler an hoot like wasa wounded animale. He wake up
everbuddy inna house. Well to wake up Pappa was like to
wake up the dead, and so up come Pappa like a ghost. He
grab my brother inna arms and care him down to the stable
where wasa donkey, horse anna goats. He tie my brother up
and tell him if he is animale then he goan sleep where he
belong. I'mma tell you after that we all sleep with our han's
over our face so we doan wake up Pappa no more.

Nowadays they's people would call that child aboose,
but for us was joosta training. My Pappa teach us to be
responsible for evertin we do, even if wasa done inna sleep.
But you know we doan know what was like to work like him.
Even when I have kids I doan work so hard. That man give
everting to us. And the only think he want from us is joosta
lissen a him and do what he say without askin the questions. I
did and boy how I use to complain, under my breath, cause
if he woulda hear me then wouldabeen a sore face for some
days.

I never did unnerstan why he was thata way until I get
marry an 'ave a my own kids. Is like the old saying: "By the
time I unnerstan that my Pappa wasa right, I have a son tell
me I'mma wrong." Come ci fa? What you goan do?

Las time I see my Pappa was day before I was leave for
La Merica. That night wasa big festa inna town for all the
boys that was leavin for Napoli the next day to catch the
boat. Wasa big party all night long. He wasa little too much
with the vino and he dance a craze tarantella with me. When
it finish he pick me up, hugga kiss me and then go home.

The nex' day when I leave. I could no fine him a
nowhere. I look inna field, I look inna olive grove. I ask
Mamma where could he be? Wasa gettin late and if I look
some more I miss the ride to Napoli. Mamma say I better
go. So I leave. Onna my way to town I was walk by the
field and there he was way off onna hill. I call out for him,
but he doan turn around. He joosta keep work. I havea no

time to go to him. Maybe is what he want. My Pappa wasa always a teach me someatin. Happa Fadda's day Pappa.

FOURTEEN — JULY, 1986

"E' finita La Merica. La Merica si
acconza e si usata. Chi non sa lavorare
va in La Merica e si va a imparare."

When I wasa boy the people inna home town say these
allatime. Is some old sayings now, but were new back then.
La Merica is the end. Once you get used to be in America,
you all used up. Those who doan know how to work go to
America an' learn.

Wasa alla time big fights about what happen when you
go to La Merica. You know back then, La Merica was like a
big story town. Whenever someone go to La Merica we never
expect to hear from them again. Whena somebuddy come
back they tell us whatever they want. Some say wasa gold
inna streets and they got lights so you can dig all night long.
Some say wasa dream land. And when we ask why they
come back they tell us that it wasa not they dream.

They use to say that once you go in La Merica you wife
won't eat pasta no more. And someatime they wasa right.
They was days we wasa luck to have bread. But we work
hard and our kids doan have it so bad as we did.

Back in my village they was old shepherd who never been
to La Merica, but he know everting about it. He say,
everyone in La Merica wasa poor.

The ones who have been in La Merica use to argue with
him in the cantina. They would tell him of the tall scrape
skybuilding, the big cars, the fact-trees where everbuddy
have work, and all the good things the rich people have.

The shepherd say, "The more a man get himself away
from the land, the more he get away from his soul. If you

take a tree from the ground it will soon become weak, shrivel up like an olive and die. Even if you have a chance to put the roots down in the ground, it won't be the same tree. The fruit will fall and waste away. 'Cambia la terra, cambia la fortuna.' Change the land and you change your fortune."

For some of us was change from bad to good, for others was no such luck. But 'come ci fa,' what you goan do. Prett soon everbuddy forget what was like to come 'ere onnaboat, to have so much trouble joosta because we look for a better life. But that is what everbuddy come 'ere for, no?

Anyway I think is a good thing to clean up that old Statue of Libertà. She was a look pretty old. But you gotta remember isa not just the way you look that counts, but is what you do. Maybe after we get that Madonna di Libertà all clean up we can start to clean up what she stand for.

You know some of our people use to call the Fourth of July, il forte gelato; the strong ice cream. Is funny no? But that is the way people think someatime. Oh yeah, I hear is even write inna book, La Merica by a good professor boy of ours Michele La Sorte. He tella a story of how was like to leave the old country. If you doan believe old Pete, joosta look in the book youself.

Anyway I hope you all havea good time celebratin this holiday and remember us old timers.

"Legno vecchio meglio brucia,
ma incenerisce prima."

That's a good old saying mean, "Old wood isa best to burn,
but quick make ash." Now you goan say, what's old Pete
tellin us now. I'mma gonna tell you a story and let you t'ink
on that.

Joosta few days ago wasa walkin in the procession of La
Festa Madonna. I wasa mindin my own bizaness, say the
prayers, sing the song, walk along, when I 'ear somea shout.
Now firs' I doan pay attention to what was go on. I mean if
somebuddy wanna shout, let them; who am I goan stop
them. I'mma no police.

Anyway, this shoutin she doan stop an now I can't
concentrate for to pray so I open my eyes and what do you
t'ink I see.

I see old Mrs. Rosalia shakin a fist at this young girl.
They wasa hollerin back and fort' and they stop marchin.
Was a big crowd aroun' these two. Now I doan like to see
so much trouble, specially inna sacred parade. So I go over
to Rosalia and ask what isa problem.

Now this old Rosalia I know her since she was a leetle
girl just come over from the old country. She wasa marry
and have many kids. One of her kids very sick soon to die.
So she pray to the Madonna, sayin that if her child lives she
goan walk in procession inna bare feet. Well to make a long
miracle story short, her leetle girl live. Doctor say was
impossible, but they always say that when they doan wanna

show how stupid they are, so I doan pay much attention. Let Rosalia believe.

Anyway, for the past seventy years there she is march in that procession senza scarpe and never once have you heard a peep out of her until this day. So I'm t'inkin must be someat'in to get old Rosalia all rile up. So I step in between the two. Rosalia wasa yell in Italian and this girl wasa all red in a face, like was full of vino. I thought old Rosalia was gonna punch this girl and that this girl was maybe gonna kick that leetle lady. So I take Rosalia to my side.

She say, "Pete, I tell you what is a problem, that leetle strega. She march in the procession, just to show her legs to all the boys. She lift her skirts and look for all the boys, then she smile. I tell her to stop, but she calls me names and tells me to go back to the old country.

"Can you believe that? Iffa we did go back to the old country, this monella would never live to let her knees be seen in daylight. I can no believe these kids. They think this is just a big parade to walk like a big shot or to show off to the boys. Madonna mia, what have we come to."

Now I tell you I know joosta what she mean. La Festa Madonna is not like used to be. People try to make bigger firecrack, bigger lawn shrine than the other, and everthing joosta bigger than everthing else. That's what La Merica can do to somethin nice. You doan stay happy with leetle things in this country. Everthing got to be improve. Well I doan know how you gonna improve on prayer. I mean until they put it inna bottle, it's gonna be joosta you talkin to la Madonna or to God or to all the saints. And the more you try to make things better, the farther you go away from what they really mean.

That young girl that make Rosalia so mad is not to blame. Maybe she thinks this procession is a parade like on 4th of July or Thanksgiving. But it's only us oldtimers who know that they's two different things. One is for show off, the other is for prayer.

Was a big deal back in the old country to walk with la Madonna an maybe is why Rosalia burn up so. Anyway, with all we have to give thanks for, let's make sure these feste doan joosta go up in smoke.

SIXTEEN — SEPTEMBER, 1986

"Con un bicchiere di vino, si fa un amico." That mean, with a glass of wine you make a friend. And I say with a glass of homemade wine, you make the best friends. I doan know if so many people make wine in they bashument these days likea we use to, but I doan think so. Our young kids got wine cellars these days, not wine barrells. I doan even know if so many people drink vino like we use to, an maybe is a problem we should talk about.

"Buon vino fa buon sangue," means good wine makes good blood. That is what wine is, it is like our blood. Now I doan mean we all gotta become alkaholic. Is only good for the old timers like me who got no more job, who live on a pension, then we can get drunk whenever we want and no one can say beans to us.

Or when you young and you just testin out to see how much you can drink. Is good to get drunk, then you know, if you can remember, how much you can take. You got to learn your limits when you young. Then you can either break them or stay with in them, but first you gotta know them. Anyway. I knew a man who would never get drunk, no matter what.

He would have contest with whoever want. Young or old he drunk them all under the table. Later on, I ask him what was his secret. He tell me, but say not to say a word to anyone until after he died. Well he died a few years ago an I never tell no one. I wait for a while joosta for to see if he was really gonea stay in that grave. Now I guess is safe to share his secret.

He say that to get ready to drink a whole lot of vino, is like getta ready to build a house. You gotta lay in a good foundation, something that will be strong, but still let the vino drip slow into the blood.

So first he would drink a half glass of olive oil. Then he would eat up some ricotta, then he would eat some hard bread and on that he would add more ricotta. Then he could go and drink even a gallon of wine if he want and if was a long contest, he would stop ever now and then to eat some bread dip in olive oil.

He say that no matter what he would never get drunk. That vino woulda drip, drip, drip into his stomach that would be like an hour glass.

Wasa big problem with wine when we come to this country. Wasa no place to get the grapes, then to stomp them, and store the mash. I'mma tell you I doan know how we did it.

Then, come the Prohibish days. They was some craze people goan try to tell us we can no drink vino. I'mma tell you I coulda been thrown in the jail many time for break that law and I doan care. To tell me that I can no drink my vino was like to tell a fish he gotta swim onna sand, or tell a bird he gotta start fly in a water. Is a real craze.

They tell us we can only make enough for to drink all by ourselves. But who can do that. Wine was not meant for to drink alone. I doan know what was in this country's mind, but they wasa no thinkin right to try to take my wine away from me.

But anyway, if you still make wine, then I wanna ask you somethin. What is you secret to make good Italian wine here in La Merica? I been livin here for a long time an I never taste a good wine like in Italy. Oh, they's a lotta good vino boys that come close, like at the Cultural Center picnic, but is still not like I use to get.

Even the wine that is import no is the same. I think they never let the best out of that country. Well it's September and for us wine makers is time to go to the track or wherever you go and buy the new grapes. And to try to make another batch.

So good luck and remember to drink with some friends. "Chi non beve in compagnia o è un ladro o una spia." Mean who doan drink in company is either a thief or a spy.

SEVENTEEN — OCTOBER, 1986

Old Mr. Colombo cross a lotta water to get over to this place. An I was t'inkin' that as long as I live water seem to be a big problem.

"Acqua di notte, pericola di morte." That's a somet'in' my old aunts used to say. It mean, water at night, danger to die. I'mma always try to unnerstan those words. Did she mean if you drink water in the middle of the night, you goan die? Or if you go swimmin or sailin at midnight you goan drown? Who knows. It's a good thing old Columbo didn't listen to that saying or he never woulda made it over here.

Nowadays people can fly over the water, but when I comeover 're we was joosta like Colombo. Let me tell you, riding those boats across alla that water was no parade. We was a shaking like olive leaves in the middle of the storm. And wasa babies cryin when they mammas was hangin over the side, given back to the ocean the cheap soup they give us.

If there wasn't so much water in the world, we could joosta walk over here, or ride some horse and buggies.

They was a boy onna boat with us who was comin to La Merica to bring his brother back to Italy. Seems his brother was stayin in America too long and his father want him back to work on the farm. That man didn't want to come onna boat, and at the dock his father was chasin him up the ramp with his horse whip.

This poor boy was real craze for to ride the boat. He say that is no good to move from one place to another, specially on a boat. When you go far away, you never come back the same. An he was right. Anyway, all the trip, he was sit in the bottom of the boat, inna dark corner. He would wake up, drink enough wine to fall back sleep and keep doin that until the boat stop.

Now I couldn't do that. I stay up onna ship as much as I can, cause I didn't wanna miss nothin. Of course, they was nothin to miss, joosta lot of water and a lotta sky. And some days you couldn't tell what was water and what was sky. They was all one bigga color. But was a big difference between the people who were up onna top and those who stay inna bottom.

Somea those who stay below say they was scared to fall offa boat. Somea those who stay on top say they wanna know iffa boat go down. Some like dark, some like light. Some travel with they eyes open, some with they eyes closed. And I guess that how most people are.

Anyway that wasa first and last ship I ever go on. I doan ever want my feet to leave the ground. Even when I sit down, my toes gotta tap the earth or I find another chair. Is joosta way I am. I doan go up inna sky, I doan go onna waterboat, an I doan take no elevators.

I guess they say the new Colombos are those who go up inna spaceboats and maybe someaday they gonna find a newland, maybe name it after some other mapmaker, but if they do, it means they's gonna be a whole lotta people that goan leave this country to go up there. An maybe then they goan know what it feels to be people likea me an all my paesani and friends who come from all over the world, in all kinda boats joosta for to live in this land. I hope they doan forget what it's like to have they feet on the ground, all the while they float inna space.

Anyway I wanna say Happy Colombo day to all my people and tell you that before Colombo could have come all the way over here, he had to travel far inside his mind and that's what the celebration should really be about.

EIGHTEEN — NOVEMBER, 1986

The other day wasa little a chilly in my place, so I go downsteers to put on a heat. Puttin' on a heat is like a big ceremony for me. It means is time to get ready for winter. An whenever I do this, I must to remember what was like back inna old country, when we don't have a switch to t'row on for to make the house warm.

When I was growin' up we use to t'row the axe against the wood for the heat. Was like flippin' a switch, not with you fingers, but with you arms anna 'ole body. Wasa hardwork. An whenever was cold, was no problem for more heat, you joosta go swing the axe, or take a walk, or keep movin for to heat up youself. I call it inside heat. You make youself warm by gettin ready to make the house warm.

Now people all think that everyt'ing is joosta sunshine an warm in south Italia, but can get pretty cold there. I remember one time wasa so cold alla olives turn black and all from the tree like was some hail storm from hell. Wasa so cold that we had share the wool with the sheep. My brothers use to go sometime to sleep inna stalla. Is funny how good we did without all this fancy way to heat up.

Now doan take me wrong. I got no gripes about my fancy furnace, is joosta that I doan have no control either. An I have some problem getting warm from invisible heat. Afterall in Italy, when we make heat, we see what we wasa burn for to make it. Sure was smoke go up inna sky, an someatime inna house, but was heat we would see and feel.

Anyway, after I flip the switch for the furnace, I go back upasteers and fix myself a little glass of new wine, joosta for to warm up the inasides. Well I was sittin there, happy to be warm, when all of a sudden the warm air she stop to blow from the vents.

So I go back down the bashument and I touch the pipes and what you think, per baccho, was cold likea ice. So I checka fusea box and was a dead fuse in there, all closed up like a black eye.

No bigga problem, I say, joosta take out the old fuse and put inna new one. When I do that, I hear the whoosh from the furnace, and the pipes start to warm up.

Well I wish I could stop my story here, but as soon as I get upa steers and sit down to watch a little televish, the warm air stop. By now I'm gettin hot like the fuse. So I go backa down and do it all over again.

Well this someonagun, she just keep blowin up, like we was havin a big argument. So I go down an tell the furnace, all I want from you is some heat, you better stop blowin the fuse or I'mma do somethin you goan regret.

I was thinkin, now what I'mma goan do to this thing. She just don't wanna give me some heat. I'mma get really steamed now and gettin all warm just from gettin so mad. I didn't know what to do, so I call up the heat man, and he says to forget about it for tonight, just bundle up and he takea look in the mornin.

Gonna cost me some money to have him come over to look at this ciuccio of a furnace. But what can I do? I'mma get so use to this mechanical heat, that I forget how to make myself warm without it. So I wrap my blanket around me and sit down to t'ink. That's when comes to me what we use to do back inna old country.

So I wonder now, effa ever people gotta do without this invisible heat, what they goan do? Come ci fa?

I hope you doan have the problems with you heat that I got, but if you do, take some advice from an old timer like me, when a fuse blow out, it means you take in too much power, give up a little an maybe you won't have such a fight with the furnace.

NINETEEN — DECEMBER 1986

"Natale con i tuoi, Pasqua con chi vuoi." That means: Spend Christmas wit you family and Easter wit whoever you want. Lemme tell you is really someatin' to be widout you family at Christmas time. It wasa my first time away from home when I come to this country. Was in October that I come to Chicago. I had joosta address of a border house. It was not so bad and after a while I was gettin use to livin in that room with three other guys like me.

Well along comes Christmas time and I was out of a job. The ground we was diggin get so hard they goan need dynamite to break it. So the boss says we don't need you wops no more. Go home. Well I was t'inkin would be nice to go back to Italy, but there was no money left after I send my family some, and I start lookin for more work, but all I fine was other people lookin for work. Wasa so bad that my paesani was joosta stay in the room and sleep all day and all night.

Well comea night before Christmas and through all the border house, the bed bugs wasa bitin even Louie the louse. Our trousers was hangin by the window sill, we had to clean them ourselves cause we couldn't pay the bill. Now I was sitting there onna my own little cot, wishin I was home, t'inkin of Italy a lot. And Nunzio was drinkin his old vino red, that he bought for a quarter from the man in the shed. Tony wasa snorin in bed already, cause tomorrow he work cause he had it steady. The streets they was empty except for the snow, and was so much of that stuff that nobuddy can go. So I pull down the shade to make it dark, cause the light come in from across the park. I lay down an think all about home and how can it be that I'm so alone. Was so quiet you could hear the mice in the wall and the water drippin out in the hall.

Now me I was joosta gonna sleep and wake up tomorrow with nothin to eat. And Nunzio he was goan go for a walk, cause we had nothin for more to talk. Louie he was gonna go to mass, joosta for to be with some lass. And Tony wasa still snorin likea big jackass. When close to sleep I finally come, wasa rap onna roof da-dum da-dum. I jumpa from the bed and roll up the shade, and a light hit my face so hard, I needa firs' aid. I keep blinkin and thinkin must be a machine that shine like the sun, but was not what I seen.

Was a river of candles float down the street, connect to the people with no shoes on they feet. They was comin from church and singing a song, and a voice call for me to join along. Well I look to see Tony still snorin away and I say to myself, 'eh is Christmas today. And joosta like back in old Italy, was Befana herself leadin the sea. I saw mamma and pappa and nonno Nicola and the oldtimers who use to play la briscola. Wasa nonna Marie and her sisters three and my brothers and cousins all wavin to me.

This I couldn't believe what I see, so I head down the steers, hurriup one-two-tree. No shoes, no socks, just trousers and me. When I get to the bottom, I t'row open the door, but the streets wasa empty, not like before. So I rub my face with the snow from the ground. And take another look, but no one was around. Now you might think I wasa crazy boy, who just make a dream, but I tell you wasa so real it seem. I seen them all paradin down there and Befana was smilin and shakin her hair. Well I holler down the street, "Hey where did you all go?" but alla I got was some more of that snow. It covered my face as I looked at the sky and froze the tears I was tryin to cry. Well I'mma no fool; I know when to give up. So back to the steers and I headed up. I fall in my bed and was soon fast asleep. The morning she woke me so hard

I had to get up. And when I went for my shoes, they was all fill up. With tarralle and pane and Christmas dolce, so what you goan do, what more can I say.

If you doan believe me, that's you problem. Wasa nice way to be with my own. Buon natale e felice capodanno.

TWENTY — JANUARY 1987

"Quando fa freddo, non stare in beddo. Quando fa caldo dorme più longo." That's an old time t'ing we used to say. "When it gets cold don't lay around. When it gets hot, you like to sleep a lot." It's not very good italiano, but is our funny mix of English an Italian. There is always plenty of t'ings to do inna summer, but is not the time to get so much done.

Now the winter, she'sa summatin else. Is really the time when you gett get you blood movin o she's a goan freeze right up in you. Funny how those saying stay with you no matter how long you life. And the reason they do is because they make good sense.

Like another t'ing we use to say: "Dove c'è il ghiaccio, c'è lo specchio." That means, "Where there is ice there is the mirror." This was something that make me think a lot.

Who do you suppose thought that saying up? Maybe was someone trying to shave they face in the cold. Or maybe was some philosopher type who found out that if you look into ice you see you own self: cold and stiff. That's what the winter can do to you if you let it.

Now it has taken me years to get used to the cold winters that we have in this country. I can't tell you how many times I curse this bitter cold and think about going back to my homeland. And if it wasn't for those old sayings, I think I would have done that long ago. Because I think what that proverb about the ice being a mirror really means is that when it gets cold enough for liquid to stay still, then maybe it's time for some self-reflection — a little bit of lookin into the ice.

Every Janwary people make up resolutions about they lives. Some gonna stop doin the things that are bad for you and start doin some good things. All that comes from our Roman days, when the god Janus was celebrated. He's the one who has two heads: one that looks forward and one that looks back. This thinkin about you life a little more than you do the rest of the year comes from him. But is more than that. We should not just think about last year, but the whole of our past. Is a time to connect ourselves with where we come from and how we get to where we are today.

The cold weather makes you bundle up and surround youself with things that make you warm. As my old Uncle Giacomo used to say, "Nothing keeps you warmer than thinkin warm thoughts," and maybe we should do more of that. Of course he's the one who also said. "Nothing is colder than the winds of advice."

Anyway, since I'm talkin about all this reflection, I think maybe I'll tell you some of what this cold weather is makin me think about.

I'm goan try to work on things in this writing I do. When I first start this talking they was some things that bother people. My English wasn't so good and that make some people angry. Well at first I was joosta goan ignore it all, cause that was something that I hear all my life. But now that I'm doing this so long, I think maybe is still enough time in this old man's life to do domething about it. So that's one of the things I'm goan work on. Maybe I can't change the way I sound, but I'm goan try to change the way my words look. And with the help of Mr. Editor Fred, I think this can happen.

Next I'm gonna learn how to work this type machine. Then maybe I won't have to worry for other people to take down what I say. An one more thing I'm gonna do is to talk more.

I spend so much time by myself that when I see people I'm not used to talkin. I'm gonna start askin questions and tellin more stories, cause I got a life full of them and all they do is run around in my head, bumpin into each other. Maybe if I get some of them out, then there won't be such a traffic jam in my mind.

These are all my plans, but as a wise old woman use to tell me: "When you make plans, expect change, but when you make change, make sure it's exact. Ma come ci fa, what are you goan do? Eh!

TWENTY-ONE — FEBRUARY, 1987

"Fesso chi fa il figlio meglio di lui," that's an old time saying that means, "It's a fool who makes his kid better than himself." That is what my people use to believe and that's why I never had a chance to go to school. My father was a tougha man who believe the only way to live is to work with you hands. He teach us everything he know and expect us to carry on his work. And when we make a mistake, he teach us with his hands not to do it again. You know something, my old papa was a no fool because we never became much better than him. But when I come to La Merica I find it would be a different thing for my kids.

If I woulda had my way, I'm sure my kids would be joost likea me. But this La Merica has a way of takin' everything you born with and changing it around. "Per prendere una cosa nuova, si deve lasciare in dietro una cosa vecchia." That means, "To get something new, you have to leave behind something old."

That's why my father woulda had a hard time in this country. He knew if he tried to make us better than himself, then we would not be so close to the land. He also think that we kids ould lose our respect for him if we put ourselves above him.

And so it was for my kids. La Merica is a place where you can no help but become better than you parents. An everyone want it that way. But I ask myself, what ways are we better off than them. Sure we got a nice home, and cars to go wherever we want, and money to do things once we get there, but does all this make us better people? I don't know, do you?

Anyway, I was thinkin of all this as I'm gettin ready to go to my first day of school. Yest, that's right, old Pete is goin to school for the first time in his life. Doan ask me why; maybe is because since I start talkin these stories for the paper I realize that nobody want to listen to some old man who can't speak English too good. Or maybe is because I'm realize that when your body gets too tired to do so many things, is time to make your mind do the work.

All us old timers got to do with our minds is remember all the good and bad times we had. I was thinking that maybe now is a good time to start thinkin about other things. I got so much time these days to do things and I don't think I'm goona be leavin so soon so maybe is time to do some of the things I never had a chance to do when I was comin up. So for my New Year's resolution I say pack up my pride and sign up for school.

My kids think I'm a craze and on the night when my class start they all come over for dinner. When seven o'clock comes they put me inna car an drive me off to school. Was funny thing to see them all wavin to me; why I think I even see a tear in my boys eyes when they drop me off. I have to tell you I was so full of nerves that my hand was a shake when I walk into the schoola room.

The place was filled with all kinda people. Was nobuddy born there in this country. Seem to me like a big minestra. They was more languages there then onna UHF televish. I thought maybe I was inna wrong place.

Since I doan know nobuddy, I take a seat in the back and wait for the teach to come in. When she come in all the people become quiet. She tell us her name and say all of us is goan learn to speak, read and write good English; that's when I knew I must be inna right place.

Then she tell us to stand up, say our names and tell something about us and why we wanna go to school. I was so surprise to see so many people havea trouble with the English like me.

When I tell them I wasa retire and talk stories to the newsapaper they was all amaze. The teach say, "If you can write, why do you take this class?" An I say, "I doan write, all I do is talk and they write the stuff down. I doan even know if they put in what I say or change things, because I doan read so well.

She laugh and say, "Most peole learn to read and write before they become writers, but you, Mr. Baffo, you do joosta opposite."

She make me feel good, because I wasa the oldest in the class. An then she say we gonna tell a story and write it. The first homework was to write somethin about our education and so this is what I write.

Mr. Editor Fred was amaze when he come to get my story this month. And I hand it to him already in writing. Sure was lot of mistakes, but this is the first thing I write all by myself. Now I'm goona try to read more and write more and fill my head with things I never know. It make me feel good that I can do these things. They say you can't teach an old dog new tricks, but not this dog.

All this reminds me of another old thing we use to say, "Chi cammina con lo zoppo, impara a zoppicare." That means, "Whoever walks with the lame will learn how to limp." And I think for too long I wasa limpin.

"Chi va a scuola dell'obbligo, sempre viaggia solo." That's a old time saying that means, "Whoever goes to forced school will always travel alone." Now I used to think I know what this means. Back when I wasa grown up only was a few kids, mostly the sick kids, who go to obligatory school. And they never had many friends cause was only a few of them in school. So it was like they was goin on a voyage by themselves.

Until joosta few weeks ago I never did spend much time in school. In fact, the last time I was in school was over sixty years back and that was for joosta few days. So now that old Pete is back in school I fine myself lookin back on all I learned in life and I begin to think twice about it all. Like with these proverbs.

Those were words that educated us. None of us used to believe that going to school had anything to do with life. Back then school was joosta for people who could afford the time to sit and learn to read. And in those days they wasn't so much to read. So school wasa biga waste of time. And when the governo di Italia tell us all we have to go to school my father put his foot down. He say, "If they goan try to take my kids away from me then, I'm goan take my kids away from them." And so that's when we moved out of the town and onto the land.

When I come to this country wasa big surprise for me when the government tell me the same thing, you gotta send you kids to school. Now I wasa so mad that at first I was goan tell the governo that we didn't have no kids, but because they live such a different life here, they was nothing for my kids to do. Stay at home, play in the streets or go to school. So my wife she beg me, "Please Pietro, let you kids go to school. They joosta goan get in trouble if you don't."

So I give in and send them all to school. But then they come back from school and tell me they goan stop to speak Italian, I wasa so mad. "Who are they to tell my kids they can no speak they own language?" I was so mad I march down to the school and was ready for a big fight. Now back then I didn't speak sucha good English like I do now. So when I meet the teach was no way for me to tell her what I think. I had to go back home and bring my oldest boy for me to translate.

Now have you ever had to argue through a translator? I'm tellin you it's not the same. You got to wait for something to yell at and then wait again for your words to fight back. It's no fun to fight that way. Is too much building up steam and lettin it seep out instead of to explode. That's when I decided we gotta learn this language. Cause how we gonna defend our rights if we speak one language an the police and teachers and politicians speak another?

Well, was one thing for my little kids to go to school, but was no way for me to go. I learn the language for the people I work with. Was only one problem. When it came to reading I was in big trouble. I had to depend on other people. How could I tell if the lawyer was not foolin me when we bought our house, or if the taxman was takin me for a fool?

As long as I had my kids around, understanding was not so hard. All the time I was thinkin of that old saying and find out that those sayings change when we come to this country. "Chi non va a scuola, non mai puo viaggiare solo." That's my new old saying that means, "Whoever doesn't go to school can never go anywhere alone."

So now I'm tryin to go to school. It's been three weeks since I started these night classes and already you can tell the difference in my words, eh? Let me tell you I still talk like I used to, but you can't tell so much in the writing, no?

It's a whole new world for me now that I can put down my own words. Oh, don't think old Pete is a genius student. My teacher correct all the mistakes I make and believea me they are so many. But I'm learning that in writing you can do things you can't do in speaking. You can hide in writing, like when a woman paints her face. You can take old wrinkles and make them disappear; you can make yourself more smart. You can do so many things.

But now I think back to that old saying and think maybe is true after all because when you read and when you write you have to stay by yourself. Is a hard thing for me to sit still when I read or write. I fine I always wanna move my hands when I talk; how can you do that and write at the same time?

An another thing, you travel in your mind more when there's no one around and maybe that's what that old saying means. If you go to school, then you learn to travel alone. Chi sa? Well pretty soon I'm goan have my examination so I better study hard. Next time I tell you how I do.

Twenty-Three — April, 1987

I got some abad news for you. Old Pete has become a statistica. That's right. I'm joosta numero in the minus column. Iffa .you doan know what that mean let me tell you simple. Moustache Pete is a dropout! That's right; a night school dropout. And to tell you the truth, I'mma happy man for it all.

I doan know what I was thinkin about when I try to go to school. I mean I have the right idea, you know; I'm old retire man with some time on his fingers and so I think maybe I could make up for some lost education. But instead of trustin my first instincts, which tell me not to go to school but to learn some new things on my own, I went ahead to this evening school.

Now if you read last month then you know everything was goan pretty good. The teach she was helpin me with my mistakes when I write. And even I was getting to read a little bit better. Well then something happen that make me really craze. We was workin on reading and come my turn to read out loud.

We was reading from some workbook about how some poor boy come in La Merica offa airplane and get lost. He could no speak English and alla time was askin for help. But no buddy unnerstan him. Now this poor boy was talk to a police man when came my turn to read.

Well I wasa pretty nerves and was a little bit shaking in my hands. I start to read and the teach say, speak a little louder. So I raise up my voice and continue to read. Then the teach, she stop me again and say, "Please Mr. Baffo, stop putting letters in the words that aren't there."

And I say, "Well scusa me Miss Teach, but I doan know what you talkina bout." And she say, "Don't you hear yourself. Everytime you say a word, you but an "A" in between. Likea thisa. Anda that'sa not a righta."

I say, "Listen, is no my fault; I can no read the langueech chop, chop like my lips was scissors an my toungue wasa knife. I likea when the language she flow smooth. Besidesa I-a doan-a read-a the-a words-a like-a that-a. Sure every once in a while a few sounds get thrown in, but that's joosta the way I am."

And then she starts to get mad. She says, "Well the least you can do is try. That's the way English is and if you don't even try, you shouldn't bother to come to these classes."

Well I tell her I promise to try, but no matter what, I fine I can no do it. So she sit me down.

Well I was sittin there and when class was over she come to me and say, "Listen, Mr. Baffo, you need to work on pronouncing. You can't sound the English language like that. And if I let you continue, then everyone is going to make fun of you.

I say, "Doan you worry for me. I'm use to it."

"Well then maybe this is not the right place for you," she says. "You tell me you've been coming here for all these weeks and you still can't tell that your still talking like you just got here."

Well that was too much for me and I blew up and say, "Listen, Miss Teach, you wasa not even born when I come here off the boat, so how do you know what I wasa soundin like way back then. Maybe I doan need this thing you call school. All we do is sit in here and pronounce words I can't say and read things I don't care about.

"Now Mr. Baffo, that's not the right attitude for a beginning student," she says. "Well maybe is not so right for a begin student, but I think is pretty find for an end student."

"Go ahead, " she say. "Drop out and become a statistic. Join the other fifty percent of students who do the same. Instead of being a number that counts, you're going to be a number that's counted. And for all the wrong reasons."

Now I know she was talkin silly. What do numbers have to do with learning to read and write? So I say, "Did you ever ask youself why so many people drop out of you school?"

"They drop out for many reasons," she say. "But most of those who do regret it."

"Well this is one number statistica that doan regret nothin," I say, and then I walk out saying, "Thank you for your time, but for me was like I walk inna store an forget what I come to buy."

So that's the story of my adult education. Now maybe the reason an old dog can't learn new tricks, is because the old tricks still work. Besides, is getting to be warmer the weather, and I think I see a bud on my back yard tree. And maybe, joosta maybe I'm goan back to Italy soon. Buona Pasqua a tutti quanti!

Twenty-Four — May-July, 1987

There once was a family call Fortunati. Now the mammas and papas of these Fortunatis wasa all born in afar off land call Italy. They come to La Merica way back inna 1900s. When the Fortunatis marry, they promise each other that they woulda work hard to see that they children would have everything.

As the family grow the Fortunatis fill they house with every modern thing money could buy. One day Mr. Fortunati come home from work with a biga box. The family gather in the living room where he set the box down. When he pull anew black and white televish from the box the kids clap they hands. Soon the family was spending much time together watchin the moving pictures.

One day the children see a commercial for Chef Boo-Jar-Dee macaroni inna can. They hounda they mama for days until she finally give up and bring home the macaroni from the groceria. 'After all,' she think, 'is much easier than spending a whole morning making the sauce like my mama used to do.' That night she set the spaghetti in front of the kids. They dip they forks into the piles and filled they mouths.

"Ugh! It's icky!" say the youngest.

"Mamma, why is it orange?" ask the oldest.

An' you know, wasa the only time that Mrs. Fortunati let her kids have they dessert without to finish they food.

"What you ask for is what you get. What you don't eat I doana forget," she say, and scrapea the plates into the garbage.

As the kids grow up they wasa spend more and more time in front of they televish. They watch any and ever'thing that come on: policeaman shows, sing song specials, old time movies and minestrone shows. When they wasa no watch the televish, they woulda play they favorite make believe game: "If I was on TV I'd be. . ." and each one would act like people onna televish.

"If I was on TV I'd be a gangster who never gets caught," would say Primo, the oldest.

"If I was on TV I'd be Rudolph Valentino," would say Duomo, the second born.

"If I was on TV I'd be the sexy lady," Terza, the only girl would say.

"If I was on TV I'd be a singer," Mino, the youngest would say and pretend to have an audience of swooning girls in front of him.

One Sunday, after a large family pranzo, the kids put on a show for the whole family. Each make believe to be a favorite TV person. The Fortunatis were proud of their children's performances, but the grandparents getta real worry.

"I doan like for our kids to act like TV," say Grandpa.

"Is this what LaMerica teaches our bambini?" aska Grandma.

"It teach them that us Italians are foolish," said Grandpa.

"We have to do something about this," said Grandma.

"You are all old fashioned," said Mr. Fortunati. "This is a new world you brought us to and our children will be the real Americans."

Well the years pass; The children finish they schooling, and the grandparents die. At the reading of Grandpa Fortunati's will the whole family was surprise to find that he had left them only one round trip airplane ride to Italy.

Attach-a to the ticket was an address. The lawyer read the will to the family.

"I am you Grandpa; you are my seed. I plant you here and know whatta you need. Choose one from among you to takea this trip. There you will find your inheritance. Now doan givea me no lip."

Because Primo was the oldest he was chosen to recover the inheritance. "Now Primo be careful," his father say. "Take this satchel and lock the money tight. Stay Away from strangers. An doan travel at night."

When Primo get to Italy he take a taxi to the address. He wasa think maybe he was headed to a bank, but when the driver tell him this was the place, he saw nothing but a small stone cottage in the countryside; he was thinkin must be some mistake. So he gets out and knocks on the wooden door. An old lady, older than any he had ever seen, opens the door. And Primo talks.

"Excuse me, but I am here to claim the fortune of Mr. Fortunati, my grandfather." Without a word the old lady wave for him to enter. She turn and walk to an open furnace where something wasa cooking.

"What are you doing?" he asked.

"I'ma making a soup."

"What kind?"

"Minestrone."

Primo look to a large wooden table that wasa covered with corn, barley, peas, potatoes, dandelion greens, beans, rice, and peppers. And Primo thinks 'Hey, I didn't come all the way here to watch a lady cook soup'; so he say "Excuse me mam, but I have come to claim my inheritance."

"Pazienza!" the old lady say. "You will get what you have come for soon enough. "First I'ma goan cook you a soup like you have never tasted. A taste you will never forget."

"What do you mean? All this stuff here we have in America," he say pointing to the vegetables and beans onna table."

"Of course you have, but you merde di cane doan know how to cook them. Now watch me carefully." Impatiently, Primo watch as the old lady drop the ingredients into the boiling water.

"First, we put these in," and she hold up a handful of what look like twigs to Primo's eyes. "These flavor the soup and never cook down. You doan have these in La Merica."

After a while the aroma fill the room and Primo's mouth water. "Could I have a taste?" he ask. She handed him a wooden spoon. He skimmed the spoon across the top of the pot and taste the soup.

"Ugh! It sure smells better than it tastes. It tastes like hot water!"

The old lady take the spoon from his hand.

"You must stir the spoon in the pot and then dip it deep down and then bring it to your lips. When you do this you can taste all the ingredients." She hand him the spoon and step back. He did as he was told and indeed, he tasted each ingredient in his spoonful. But there was a flavor he had never tasted before, a flavor he couldn't name.

"Old woman, what is it that makes this soup taste better than any soup I've ever eaten before? I can taste every ingredient separately and yet there is a flavor I cannot describe!"

After a long silence she take the spoon and dip it into the pot. She brought up a spoonful of the first ingredient that she had placed into the pot. She raise the spoon to his eyes. "These. They flavor, but they never boil away!"

The two sat down and ate the soup. When they finished Primo said, "Old woman, I thank you for the wonderful meal and now, may I have my inheritance. I must be going."

"But my son, you have been given your inheritance. You have what you have come for."

"What do you mean? I have nothing but a full stomach! What are you talking about?"

"Give me that satchel."

"Now she will fill it with Grandpa's fortune," he thought and smiled. But the old woman took the satchel to the wooden table and began filling it with the roots — the ingredient that looked like twigs. Primo jump from a table, "But what is this? You aren't filling this with my grandfather's fortune. What are you trying to do, cheat me out of my inheritance!"

"No, young man. This is your inheritance! You have learned how to cook the minestrone. Now I am giving you the one ingredient that you cannot find in your country so that when you cook the soup it will be the same that you have eaten today. You see, your grandfather never said your fortune was in gold. He was a smart man. He knew that more than money, you need to eat well. You need not to forget how to cook so that each ingredient remains unique, but when combined with all the rest gives a new flavor to the soup."

Well Primo didn'ta know what to do. He wasa so upset that all he could do was to take the suitcase from the oldwoman and sit down to cry. She shuffle over to him and say, "Why you crying, my poor boy?"

"I know my family is going to be mad at me. They were expecting me to bring home Grandpa's fortune and now when I get home all they're gonna see is this bag full of sticks."

The old woman shake her head and stand up. "Come with me; I wanna show you somea things."

Well Primo follow her out the door and she lead him over to the fields.

"You see this land. This was where you Grandpa wasa born. I know him since he wasa baby and watch him grow up.

Even when he was a littlea boy he wasa work everday to help
his Mama an Papa. It wasa sad day when he leave for La
Merica. He was joosta kid. And you know he promise
everone that he would come back someaday. Oh he send a
lot of money home to his family; they was able for the first
time to own they own land. You see his hard work in La
Merica made his family like the borghese. But they was
always wait for you Grandpa to come back, but he never
did."

"But what does all this have to do with our inheritance?"
ask Primo.

"You're not listening? This is you inheritance. This and
the ingredients I give you for the soup. Now you listen to
me. You go back to La Merica and cook for you family the
soup like I show you. When they eat it and listen to your
story they will understand everything."

Primo leave Italy all confuse and was a worry for his
father to yell at him for being robbed out of their
inheritance. When he get home the family think he go crazy
from the Italian heat when they see that he had come home
with nothing more than a suitcase full of roots.

"What'sa wrong with you, my boy?" yell Mr. Fortuna.
"How can you be so foolish as to settle for this box of roots
when you should have had your Grandpa's inheritance. He
work his whole life and do you think he did it all for this?"

Primo remembered what the old woman said and before
he try to answer his father he hurry into the kitchen. Ever'one
was laugh when they see him tryin to cook the soup. But as he
cook he tell them what the old woman say. No one believe
him until they taste the soup he make. Then they all agree
that the trip had beena worthwhile. And the Fortunati family
ate well ever after, never forgetting that it was the roots that
make the soup unique.

And that's the end of my story.

Twenty-Five — August, 1987

The last three months I was writin to you a story about an Italo American boy name Primo. Well finally that story is finish. I hope you like it and that it make you think some about what us Italiani are doin in this country. I did get some letters from you that was askin for some 'splanation of it, but I think if you read them all togedder then maybe is no need to 'splain. That's what I hope.

Anyaway, this month I'm gonna talk to you 'bout someathing I doan unnerstan so good. Maybe some of you can help me out. I'mma talkin 'bout baseaball. What's so big about this game that everbuddy is so craze about.

Las' week I wasa goan onna trip to the ball game with the senior citizens. Was the alderman who give us the ticks and the bus ride. I didn't vote for him so I doan think I should be goin, but my friends pull my leg a little and tell me is a good thing to do. I live in this country for more than sixty years and I never once go to the stupid game, so I think maybe is someat'ing I should do, after all they call it this country's pasta time and is about time I fine out why.

Now I've seen the games on televish, but never could I watch a whole game. Was joosta nothing going on that was so interesting to me. But is a different ball game when you go to see them onna the feel. Not that the players do anything different. Is joosta that there is so much more to see than on the televish.

When we get offa bus we go right into the ballpark. I tella you I never see so many happy people in one place in my whole life. Was like a bunch of bees buzzing around a hive full of honey. Everbuddy wasa smile and jump up an down and that was before anything even wasa goin on. Wasa so many people there and I wasa wonder why all these people doan have to work today. Had to be becoz some were so rich or so poor or so retired that they fill up a big place likea this inna daytime.

Well a younga man lead us way up to what they call a grandastand. I wasa so happy they had chairs up there because I was t'inkin isa not too grand to stand after makin that biga climb.

After a while the boys run out to play and then they sing the country song. Wasa nice to see everbuddy stand to sing the song. Then everone cheer and the game shea start. Now I doan know baseaball from a mountain of pasta fagioli, but it makea no different to me becoz was so nice joosta be in the sunshine and watch all the people watchin the game.

When I was sittin there I wasa t'inkin about how this must be how it was in the days of the Romans and the biga Colliseum. Only difference is they wasa no gladiators fightin or cristiani lettin themselfs get eat up by lions. They was some people yellin out to kill somebuddy — I think they wanna kill the bump or somebuddy like that, but I think maybe they was joosta makein the joke, becoz no buddy gonna kill somebuddy in front of alla those people. At least I hopea not.

I wasa sittin next to old man Mickey; now he's a guy who know ever'tin about this game. He was writin down evertime somebuddy do somethin. I ask him, whatta you doin. And he tell me he'sa keepin the score. I doan unnerstan why he joosta don't look up at that big board to find the score, but like I say, baseaball makes some people craze.

Mickey was tellin me that some of those guys out there is amillionairs. Now that wasa someat'in is joosta too hard for me to believe. How come they makea so much money just to play this funny game? Iffa I woulda known that then maybe I woulda try to learn this game when I wasa kid. In one year some make more than I did in my whole life. Incredibile! I know it must be hard to keep shakin that stick at a ball that is flyin at you face, but why is it worth so much; can it be that the game is so dangerous?

Anyway that game go on for a long time. One time everbuddy stan up to singa another song and I wasa t'inkin' wasa gonna sing the country again, but they fool me. They all singa someat'in calla "Takea me outa to a ballagame." A big man was leanin out of the window box, leadin everbuddy to sing. Mickey tells me the guy was some Italiano name Harry. When I hear him sing, I say to Harry, "Scusa me buddy, but no Italiano singa that bad."

One ofa the things they say in the song is "I doan care if I ever get back." Now I'mma tell you, is not such a bad place to be for an afternoon, but I'mma one guy who cares if he gets back home. I know a lot of paesani make good by playin this game, but this is one Italiano that's gonna leave this game to the 'mericani. Hope you all havea nicea summertime; maybe I'll see you at le feste.

TWENTY-SIX — SEPTEMBER 1987-APRIL 1988

Summat'ing very strange happen to me lasta month. I t'ink is goan change my whole life.

My old friend Angelo pass away in his sleep one night. He wasa 87 years old and wasa my friend since we wasa boys. We comea over here together inna 1920. I wasa so sad for to hear about his death. Ma come ci fa. He had a good life and died a happy man, what more can you aska for, eh?

Anyway, the day after I hear about his death I get a call from his lawyer, he tell me he wants me to come for to hear the reading of poor Angelo's will. So I get dress up and go downtown. I was sittin inna big leather chair so high up in the sky that I can see the whole city out from the window.

Wella the lawyer man began to read the will and old Angelo was very generous. He leave some money to his family and somea to his church. I was wonderin why I had to come downtown when all of a sudden I hear, "And if by chance my old friend Pietro Baffo should survive me, and if he should be in good enough health, I want him to bring me back to Italy. For that I leave money for his round trip ticket and enough to cover my funeral, burial and perpetual care of my grave. He always told me we should go back home before we die and maybe this will be his chance."

At first I didn't believe my ears. Then the lawyerman show me the writing and tell me that all the arrangements are being made and we leave in two days.

Now I'mma tell you I was no ready for this news. Is been too long since I been back inna old country. And sure I t'ink alot about goin back, but not like this. I doan even know if they is anyone back inna our village who remember me. Besides I didn't even havea the passaport for to travel. But the lawyer says not to worry, some friends of his in government would take care of ever't'ing.

Well after a short wake and a little festa for the family here, we wasa headin out to the airport. Me in the front seat of the funeral car and Angelo layin in the back. I wasa t'inking about how me and Angelo came to La Merica together onna boat, the Stella Maria del Mare. We wasa young boys full of life. I wasa the one who was layin down the whole way cause the sea she shake my stomach so much and Angelo wasa takin care of me. And now here we are, gettin onna big aeroplane to makea trip back. Is so funny how this life turns out.

Well they load up Angelo into the place where is alla baggage and I takea seat onna plane and we fly off.

Now all this wasa not too bad. I wasa so surprise to fly all that way and not even feel a littlea bump. In less then ten hours we woulda be landin in Roma. Now I feel likea prince to come back to my old country inna jet plane, but also I wasa feelin a little afraid. Is been over sixty years since I wasa back. I didn't know what I would see.

I have to tell you thata worse t'ing of all wasa the food; wasa ever'tin inna plastic and nothin havea taste of real food. Wasa good thing I bring a little of D'Amato's bread, some Falbo cheese, and some of my wine, or else I woulda be too hungry for sure.

Wasa so nice to be inna plane with so many of my paesani. They wasa all speaking the good Italian that the people ona televish talk. I wasa surprise to see so many people goin to Italy, especially after all this terrorismo stuff that happen, but nobuddy seema to worry so much.

I even meet onea man who goesa back ever summer. He wasa tellin me how much better Italy is today and that if wasa like this years ago he would never leave. Now that is someat'in I coulda not believe. But as soon as they open the door to let us out, I wasa begin to unnerstan what he wasa sayin. Wasa whole new Italy right before my face and there's so much to tella you that I think I'mma goan be writin for a while.

Whoever was that man who say you never can go home again never tell you what happens when you try to. And that's joosta what happen to me when I wasa bringin my old friend Angelo back to be bury in our homeatown. Alla my life in La Merica I was always thinkin hard to keep alive the pictures of my Italy in my head.

You know, whenever wasa gettin too cold I think ofa those sunny days onna mountain side beach when the sun she wasa so bright I hada to keep my eyes squeeze all day long. Or like whenever it get so hot I think of that grape vine shade along sidea my house anna the only cool place inna ground under a house where my papa he keepa the vino, or the corner up onna mountain top where the wind never stop to blow.

Well what I wasa rememberin all those days was not what I see whenna train she pull into my littlea paese. I'mma tellin you at first I t'ink I wasa inna wronga place.

First I have to tell you that wasa big problema for me when I try to speak to people. Back when the plane she stop in Roma I had the trouble esplainin to the people what wasa I doin anda where I wasa goin. You see, all the time Iwasa talkin the old dialect from my village.

Back when I wasa kid we didn't go much to school and they wasa no televish or radio, so we never get to hear how wasa talkin alla other Italiani. Joosta when the people was travelin through our town did we get to hear the other dialetti. I hear and learn more Italian livin in La Merica, then I ever do in Italia. So wasa good thing for all of us from different areas to be livina near each other, but was astill not the same as bein in Italia. You t'ink I wasa speakin

English. The way they look at me when the words come outta my mouth wasa like I wasa spittin on them.

People musta think I wasa some ancient man because one lady she tell me she don't hear my way to talk since she wasa littlea girl.

I can't tell you how much scared I was to be back inna Italy. Wasa ever'tin movin so fast, joosta what I doan like in America is a happen the same over there. Wasa like somea bad dream for me. Wasa good thing I wasa with Angelo, becoza the train people take better care of the dead than they do of the live. If wasn't for the way they worry for to carry that coffin, then I'mma sure I woulda got lost and taken by some bandits. They put Angelo inna mail car and I wasa sittin in the car right behind it. No matter what I did I could no get comfortable. I wasa joosta leanin against the window.

Now wasa long time I wasa lookin outa the window before I see anything that looks alike the Italy I leave over sixty years before. Wasa so many smokeastacks and telephone wires and roads and cars and biga tall buildings and ever't'ing likea in La Merica that if ever'one wasa no speakin Italian maybe you could fool me that I wasa still inna USA.

After a few hours we get deep inna countryside and then for a little time I see someatin like the old country I remember. The sun wasa notta so bright and wasa little more haze then I remember. I wasa think maybe like iron the old country she get a little more rusty since I wasa boy, cause that wasa the color of the sunashine onna hills and the grapeyards and this was right inna mezzogiorno.

Well for a while I close my eyes and try to geta some sleep. I musta been out for a longa time because nex' t'ing I know I'ma wake becoz some buddies is screamin and at first I thought for sure I musta be dreamin becoz is the old words from a village close to mine. The trainman comes to me and tells me I better get ready becoza next time she stop is when we get off.

When my train wasa gettin a pretty close to my homeatown, I look outa window an' start to see my old countryside. Wasa joosta like I remember it. Fields full of the olive trees, so big and so twisted up. And miles of green grapeyards. And the air down close to the ground is so dusty. Wasa the sky so blue makes you think wasa paint. As I see all this I'mma start to feel not so scared, but wasa really feelina sad. I even start to cry, becoz of all the memories that come back so quick.

You know when you live a long life like me, someatimes you can hide the bad times way back in you head an never think about them; but the same can happen for the gooda times. This little trip back to my home land was likea magnet for all those times. It bring them all up to the front of my mind. Oh for years I getta the letters from the old country that tell me who marry and who die, but they was joosta words onna page that make me think of what used to be; but now I wasa goin back to see what wasa left of what had happen all those years in between. It make me think about what woulda happen if I never left this place and come to La Merica. Ma che sarà, sarà.

Well when the train she slow again and there was the name of my town written onna sign the same as it was the day I leave it goin the other way for La Merica. I look up to see my village and I could no believe my eyes. Wasa wires all fill up the sky, like my oldtown wasa wearin a lady's hair rollers or something. Even this deep inna south had comea the televish and phones. Wasa incredibile. And there at the station was a big band of paesani who have come to meet us. Wasa mix up all those faces, and on some was a smile I recall, another a nose, another eyebrows, another a hat. I was sure I knew the whole crowd, but I felt like a stranger when the people come up to my window and call for me one by one. Everone knows my name, but I doan know no one until I see one of my cousins. I let him take my bags and help me offa train. Then I lead the crowd to the baggage car where old Angelo's coffin is bein takin off.

At first alla people stay away from the bronze metal box with the golden bars. I guess they never see such a casket. Angelo's old sister wasa tellin the funeral man that she doan believe that's her brother. She was screamin at him to open it up. So guess what? Right there at the station, joosta asa the train is pullin away, the funeral man pops open the casket and the crowd all shut up. Wasa joosta the sound of the squeakin train wheels turnin. And then, the everbuddy come up around to look at Angelo. I tell you he doana change too much since I last see him inna Chicago at a the wake. Then likea crack of thunder one lady sends up a scream that would wake all the saints from they nap. Another one faints and then comes a whole chorus of moans from the paesani. The women all gather together and begin the mourning. Wasa so much that even I begin to cry, not becoz is old Angelo dead, but for all the people around me who joosta begin to know that one of they good old boys who went off to make a good, joosta come home to rest. The funeral man he close the coffin and a group of boys get it ready to move.

Well I had to say thata the walk from the station to Angelo's sister's house wasa maybe the longest walk I ever take. There was Angelo's coffin ona cart, bein pulled by a donkey and me and his sister Nina walkin behind it. Everone isa lookin at the coffin and I'm lookin at ever one. I was steppin on the same stone streets that was there when I wasa boy. They wasa joost as smooth and strong as when I was kid. Make me think of my street back inna Chicago, the one that every winter eats into Swiss cheese.

Well once we get to Nina's house, she tell everyone that tomorrow is goan be the funeral and that friends should come by tonight to see Angelo one morea time. They crowd starts to break up and little Nina asks me if tomorrow I can say somea t'ings at the services. I say doan worry and we have a big hug.

After we leave Angelo's sister's house, my cousin Nicola takes me over to his house and tells me to rest. Now I haven't seen these people for more than fifty years, and even though they my relatives, I doan know what to say to them. I can not rest so I sit up with them in they kitchen and we drink more coffee.

Everbuddy wanna know what is La Merica like. An they all wanna know what happen to all the paesani who leave our town. They think I'mma goan know the fate of every immigrant that come to La Merica from our village. Joosta because we in the same country.

Now you have to know one thing about Italians; they think that to lose track of a paesano is joosta like to kill them — maybe is because Italia is such a small country, and that you never are too far from some relative, somewhere: even if you are in Sicily and your cousin is in the Alps. But what they doan know that iffa I'mma in Chicago and they cugino is in Nuova York, that's like if one was in Russia and the other is in Ireland.

Anyway, we talk all night long and I try to explain what is La Merica and you know what my 100 year old uncle Damiano tells me? He says, it sounds like what La Merica is, is joosta what's wrong with Italia today. And isa good thing that he doan come to La Merica years ago when he hada the chance, for sure he woulda been dead as Angelo right now.

Now he make me think some. And I think maybe that old rooster he'sa right. Way back when Angelo an I leave our village, times wasa bad, and everone wanna leave; but when I look around at the old place now, it doan seem so bad. And that's why is nobuddy inna hurry to leave.

Well, I'ma tell you if it wasn't for Old Damiano's wine, we would never goan asleep. Now I doan have to tell you that the Italians makea somea pretty good wine. But what you doan know is that the best wine they make never leaves the country. It stays right there and sits in the cellars of the paesani who make it. And is no price possible to make them give it up. That's the wine that we was drinking; they call it "vino nero" — the black wine. And I tell you is nothing like it nowhere.

Too much "vino nero" will make you lights go out like wasa black out. But the wine joosta begins to work once you power's knocked out. "Vino nero" is so strong that once you unconscious, it starts to work on you subconscious.

That night I doan know how I got into the bed, but I will never forget what happen when I was in there. I hada the most incredible dream of my life.

I was walkin with Angelo, who was still alive, up the side of the hill in our village. Now it wasa the highest hill, where the Convento and the cemetery is. They sky wasa all swirl up with purple and orange. The air around us was chilly, joosta enough to make our skin bump up even under our clothes. We wasa huffin and puffin up the hill and not sayin nothin. From out of nowhere comes flyin seagulls and they start crashin into the side of the hill, like they was blind or someatin. They was comin down like was a snowfall. I turn to tell Angelo to hurry up, that we better get inside the Convento quick, when all offa sudden a bird hits him and he disappears into the hillside without a sound.

Now I wasa sure the same woulda happen to me, but even when the birds hit me was like they go right through. I doan feel a sting. I go back to where was Angelo and I see nothin but the heads of the birds, singing "Volare," joosta like inna record. I doan know what to do, so I run up to the Convento, push back the huge wooden doors and slip inside.

Now is not the Convento that I remember from bein a kid. Instead is black marble walls that stretch up to heaven filled with photographs of people I know back in Chicago. Was likea mausoleum. I wasa so scared, I cried.

The morning after that crazy dream, I get up to get ready for the big funeral day. My head was kinda puffy and felt to me likea bigga soft a tomato. My throat was likea fica d'India in Agosto and my breath was like the Sicilian scirocco sweepin through a goat shed. Sure I drink so much a that "vino nero" that I wasa sure it take the place of my blood. It make me daytime dizzy and wasa only after I washa up an shave that I start to feel my toes again.

I wasa the last one up and everbuddy else was already outside the house. The only one there at the breakfast table wasa old Signora Rosalia. She look like she wasa waitin joosta for me.

"Buon giorn'," she say, "An how did the 'merican' sleep last night."

"Notta so good," I say, and then I tell her the dream.

Now this old Signora, she must be pushin cent'anni if she's a year, but she got eyes like a little bambino. They wasa twinklin, like she know someating that I doan. I have to tell you that Rosalia is a institution in my old paese. Some say she used to eat dinner with the angels and then dance with the devil. She is the lady all the young girls see to have they dreams explained. She's the first face the new babies see as they leave they mammas. She'sa the lady the young mothers go to when they bambini got the "malocchio" and she's the one who gets the dead ready for the burial. The Church doan care too much for her (even though she's the best churchgoer in town), but she's got more power than they know how to handle so they leave her alone.

Anyway old Rosalia let me finish my caffè and then she talk.

"Oiiee Baffo Pietro," (she doan like my 'merican name of Pete), "you dream up a real good one this time. You an' poor Angelo were heading up the hill to heaven. The air was cold because you were on the path of death. The birds that come flying down at you was like the holy spirit. They go right through you because that's what religion is to you; it goes in one ear and out the other. Now when they hit Angelo, he disappears, because he's made peace with 'La Madonna' and 'Il Signore.' When you look for you friend, all you see is a bird's head and it's singing 'Volare.' Now that's the spirit telling you someday you goan have to learn to fly. You get so scared you race up to the top of the hill an run into the Convento, cause you know that's were it's safe, in the house of 'La Madonna'."

"Now when you go into the Convento, is no more like wasa when you wasa boy. Instead is like a 'casa di riposo'. That means that you own death is not so far away and you are not ready for it. You see the pictures of you friends 'mericani all up onna walls, like they was the ones buried there. That means that in Italia La Merica is dead, and in America, Italia is dead. For all this you cry because you are confused. You know the dead now on both sides of the sea."

Now when I hear these things I tell you I get a chill upa my back like wasa ice drops falling on my skin. I try to tell myself this old lady is joosta too fill up of religion, but sometings she says I have to agree with. She'sa right. I'mma not ready to die. But I guess until old Angelo's death I haven't really thought about my own.

La signora look me deep inna eyes and then she clap her hands and say, "So Baffo Pietro, that's awhat you dream isa tellin you. Is joosta a reminder that someday you gonna fly away joosta like you buddy Angelo. An you gotta start to get ready for that flight. Now I must leave and get ready to say addio to Angelino."

"Lo sciocco teme e fuge la morte, il pazzo cerca e le corre incontro, il saggio l'aspetta."

That's an old saying that the old priest say at Angelo's funeral mass. He didn't say whose words they are, but they really make me think about how I look at life.

The saying goes like this, "The fool is afraid and runs from death, the crazyman looks for it, the gatherers find it and the wise expect it."

Now that make me think of the dream I have the night before the funeral. Maybe I was alla time trying to run away from death. When I look around at all the people at Angelo's funeral I was thinkin that maybe this was someatin that I got from bein in La Merica.

You see in Italia death is right there along with life. You see it everyday. Everytime somebuddy is a die in my old home town, they have a big procession witha banda an everything. All along the streets on the walls of the buildings they put up signs that tells everyone who is dead. Death is a constant companion to those in my old town. Even today the widows wear black. And in my town they don't hide the old people away so that only they family knows when they die; they doan rush the body into the ground in speedy cars. Angelo's funeral make me know again that death is just as worthy of a celebration as is birth, a wedding or a birthday. And those words tell me that in La Merica we doan know how to work with death.

Anyway Angelo's funeral wasa someatin else. It shows you that even when you die, you're a not done spending money. They was so much money had to be spent. First there was the band, is the same band they use for le feste. Then they was the picture cards and the signs for the walls. Of course they had to give the church a little somethin. And then they was the cart for his coffin. His family save a space for him in the cemetery wall; it was the least they could do since it was Angelo's money that let them buy a bigger piece of land for to bury the relatives. Finally wasa the big festa di mangiare after the funeral, the custom where the family of the dead feed everone who comes to say good bye. In the fancy towns the family take the people a ristorante, but in our village the people still come to the house with food in they hands. Even so they was a lot of vino and food to buy.

They was no buddy ina hole town that didn'ta know that Angelo wasa dead. Even the littlea children follow the procession. Is the old ways I guess to make everbuddy a part of all that happens in life and in death.

Anyway that was how we say goodbye to my old friend Angelo, in the good old fashioned way. And it was during the meal afterwards that I come to understand how I 'ava become so different from the people who didn't leave the land like me.

We wasa all sittin around a table in the back of the house under the shade of so many lemon trees. All the old men sat together and some of those I grew up with were asking me how come me and Angelo never came back home like so many of the others. Now I really doan know why I never came back; I guess because when you stay away so long, home gets farther and farther away and pretty soon is joost another picture in you mind. Now they could no unnerstan that. And with drinkin all that vino nero we was alla gettin pretty loud and start to arguing about where life is better: La Merica or L'Italia.

Now there is no way to answer that question. There's good and bad in both. And no one can say for sure unless they live three lives: one in Italia, one in America and one some place else for to make right comparison. But I tell my buddies that is no difference where you life your life, but how you live. But after all that good wine, wasa nobuddy listening to anything but they own thoughts. Well that's the story of my friend Angelo's last trip home.

I thought this would be the end of my story of goan backa to Italia. But I have a few more tales to tell you. After we bury old Angelo my jobba wasa all done. I decided to stay a few more days, after all I wasa sure this would be my last time here.

The morning after we bury my friend I take a walk around my old village. It wasa good to see the old farmers out in they fields, a workin joosta like they always did. I maybe walk a mile or two and wasa so hot a morning that I was thinkin maybe to take a walk up into the hills for to cool off a littlea bit, like I use to when I wasa kid. And maybe find that old spring where the water was so good.

Wasa hard to climb up, harder than I remember, but for an old man I did pretty good. I wasa walkin up an old path when I hear some piping music. I knew right away had to be some of the old shepherds. I knew right where they was, cause when is hot they let they sheep graze on the shadyside of the mountain, and later, when the sun comes up to high noon, they come down a little a bit and rest in a grove of olive trees.

Now when I wasa boy, the contadini down in the valley use to tell us to stay away from the pastori, said they all was alittle funny in the head, that it come from being alone all the time with no one to talk to but the sheep. Other people said that's why they pipe the music all the time, to keep from goin craze. Anyway I use to know a boy who wasa so good he could sing and play with the angels; he wasa so good that if he would record his music I'm sure he woulda be rich and famous. He had a funny name, Titiro, that come from an old Sicilian family. When I hear the piping I was awonderin what ever happen to Titiro. He use to graze his sheep right up on this mountain.

Joosta when I wasa t'inkin of him I hear a voice sing out, so I start to walk to it. Right onna top of a hill wasa small white-haired man sittin on a rock, looking out over the other side. He wasa wearing a white shirt, a sheepskin vest, brown knee pants an no shoes on his feet.

He didn't stop pipin even when I come right up to him. He joosta look at me, wink his eye and keep on playin his pipe. I sit down next to him an look out over the land. Wasa so peaceful there. The sheep down the hillside was nibblin at the grass. The bees wasa buzzin on the flowers and from this side of the hill all we could see was olive trees, and fields. Everything was like life here never change.

When he stop it get so quiet, like the whole land was waiting for more. Even the sheep turn they heads to see why the music stop. He put his pipe in his pocket and pulled out his wine bag. He offer me some even before he knew who I was. After we drank some he spoke. Funny thing was, that even though he stop to sing, he was still speaking in song.

"So its you Baffo Pietro, and why have you come back. Have you come up to the mountain to find something you lack?"

I say, "So you still remember me, eh?"

"Of course I can remember; the boy's still in your face. Dont' forget us pastori see so few of human race."

I didn't know what to say to old Titiro; how can I tell him all of sixty years in one conversation. Joosta when I was gonna ask him how he's doin he grab his pipe and sing another song.

"We're still little boys my Moustache Pete, like roots of oak have grown our feet; I stayed in the hills and you've crossed the seas; but none can say where's better breeze. Yours at the back, mine in the face; and now we're near the end of our race. Years ago we sang of love as if life depended on it. And now my friend what can we say have we lost or found it? You've come back with stories to tell; and I've a life of songs; why don't we try our hand at finding out to whom the best belongs."

Old Titiro wasa talkin about how we use to sing together and the one who made up the besta song would win a prize.

Now I usea to be pretty good at this back when I was aboy, but I don't sing inna contest for over fifty years. My pipes wasa pretty rusty and old Titiro he wasa singin like he never age a year. There we was up onna mountain side, lookin out over the land. Wasa soft breeze comin to me uppa there and it make me feel like a kid again. Is funny what natura can do to you no matter how old you are. We sang in our old dialect, but I'll give it to you in English. I let old Titiro go first.

Oh Baffo Pietro what do you know, you come back to your home with a head full of snow. What can you say for the years you've been gone. Now tell me all in your own little song.

I tell you old Titiro, I've seen many things that the coming and going of seasons can bring. I've been poor with just pasta fagiole for to eat; and I've been rich enough to buy wine in the street.

So you've been rich and been poor in the stomach and head. But tell me where is there better the bed. Where you dream makes a difference in life don't you know; have you married? Have you children? Now this I must know.

Well my old shepherd friend I've done all that you said. I've outlived my wife and now make my own bed. Of children I've four: two boys and two girls; and they have often put me into whines and to whirls.

Children can do this, I know very well. Now tell me what have they drunk of your well. Do they all speak La Lingua and follow old ways; or have they gone to make something else of their days?

I tell you old friend it was hard when I left, to keep the old ways but I did my best. My kids understand me sometimes this I know, but they don't speak too well and they talk very slow. There's so much they don't know of what's in my head, for I never found English to cook what it's fed.

Oh Baffo Pietro you made a mistake, so much have you lost when you can't bake a cake, from all the right items in the old recipe; if you want to know why just listen to me.

You can't even know what we all went through; to become mericans there was so much to do. Some change their names; some lose the old tongue; send their children to schools that kidnap the young; schools that make them embarassed of their old family; so they all turn away from old Italy.

I can't tell you how sad your song makes me today; to think that the good gets all thrown away; just to survive and to eat like a king; tell me what was it caused all this trouble to spring.

We didn't own land; had no money to spare; so we shutup and listen, but in dreams did we dare. By the time we were fed in the body we found; we were leaving our souls to be led all around. Can you imagine that there even nature has changed; we learned darkness and snow not sunshine and rain. Our whole world turned around when we left our old land; and so we looked for work with our hats in our hand.

But now you have come back to old Italy; what say you to changes you can't help but see. There's talk of the government taking our land, to build powerful places that will run the whole land; and out they will throw us from our ancestors homes, then dig up the land disturb all their bones. I tell you old friend it's a good time to die for memories like ours can do nothing but cry.

Now that's where you're wrong my old Titiro; man changes his ways for better or good; and whose to decide between plastic and wood. The world has seen changes like never before; and what's to stop it from changing some more.

Well my friend you've sung well and I hand you my best; now go back to your land, but remember this contest.

Well wasa good to sing with my old shepherd friend and he wasa the first of many sad goodbyes I had to say; oh we both cry, because we know that we will never see each other again, but that wasa joosta the beginnin of the cryin.

When I left the hills I wasa headin backa to town for to get my things ready to go back to La Merica. In somea funny way I wasa t'inkin what woulda happen if I would nota go home; what if I joosta stay right here an send for my children to sell my house an evertin insidea it. Wasa really strange to think like that because of course I coulda never do it. Iffa I did, then those 60 years I spend in La Merica woulda be joosta like a long vacation, like a life long dream. No, I said to myself, is better to make the dream live in Italy.

Well onna my way into the town I run into an old beggarman who wasa sittin outside of a little stone hut that was all but tumbled down. I wave to him as I walk an he call me over.

Thisa man was much older than me, way over 90 at least. He still had all his hair, and dirty strings of it stuck out of an old silk cap that wasa squeeze so tight on his head so when he take off his cap wasa red ring across his forehead. He was wearing a baggy black coat like the old time politicians wear and under it an old Garibaldi red shirt. His pants wasa made up of many different pants — a little patch of black here, red there, one leg wasa striped and the other wasa solid green tweed. He was sittin with his back against the door and his legs up to his chest.

I said, "Oay, old man, what do you want?"

He say, "I want to talk to a merican," in a thick Napolitano dialect that squish the words all togedder.

"An how do you know I'm a merican?" I say inna my best paesano dialect.

"I can tell by the pants that you wear. Is no way an Italian could stay in business makin pants like that. So tell me Mister Merican. What are you doin around here?"

"I come to bury my old compare who die in La Merica?"

"If he died there then why didn't they bury him there?" said the old man with a biga laugh that show me a mouth of strong white teeth except for one missing in the middle."

"Because he said in his papers that he wants to be buried back in his home country?"

"Well that's what the rich can do then. Leave the country when times are bad; go away and make their money; then come back here when they can't live no more, hide their stinkin carcass in our beautiful land takin up valuable space."

Well I wasa gettin so tired from all my walkin that I wasn't going to start a fight with this old man. I joosta nod my head and say, "A man can do whatever he wants when he's got the money, eh?"

Well wasa the wrong thing for me to say because this man turn into fire and jump up screamin. His black eyes grow big as bocce balls and he shouts out, "No, a man with money is a slave to those who'll take it. He can't do a thing without it and he does nothin with it. Was the biggest mistake this country make when it start printing up money. You know it use to be against the law to sell bread here. No, no, no, money doesn't give a man freedom, it takes his freedom and shackles it with jobs and bills and projections."

Now I hear stories like this alla time and I was tinkin that this guy wasa really craze to begin with so I tip my hat and say I gotta be goin.

He grab on to my arm like I wasa log in a river that was sweepin him away. I couldn't believe his strength; his hands wasa like teeth. He say, like he wasa pleadin for his life, "Please signore, you must listen to my story; If I doan tell you this story I will never forgive myself. A man like you needs to hear it and take it back to La Merica before it's too late. I won't take much of your time and you'll see that it's worth more than money can buy."

He wasa so craze for to tell me thisa story that I thought wasa better idea to listen than to make him more craze. So here is his story.

"You see this trullo that's all broken down; it tells the tale of going to war, and what a man can expect to find, when he leaves his home so far behind. On this very spot there once lived Guido, a man among men, a contadino. He worked by building homes of stone; why in less than a week he could make one on his own. Now Guido was a happy man, with a wife, six kids and a prospering trade. People came from all around to see the homes he made. For a bale of hay or a bushel of crops, he would trade his skills and build a home."

"Then one day, not so long ago, the soldiers passed this way. Men with shirts as black as night, on horses and on foot. Some with guns, some with knives, some with nothing but fists in their hands. They followed a balding gentleman, who sat on his horse, commanding the clan. Guido stopped his work when he saw the troops, and walked up to the leader. 'Come join us!' he called. 'We need every able man; to fight for our freedom; to defend this fatherland.' Now Guido complained that he had too many children, to run off to war; but the leader wouldn't hear him and yelled out somemore. 'Your children need a future if they are to survive the invasion that we suffer to destroy. What good is bread without eating with pride; what good is your life when it's not satisfied; it is better to live one day as a lion than a life time as a sheep; come with us or die right here. We haven't got time, the enemy's near'."

Now Guido was moved by all this talk. He looked to his wife and then to his kids, then said goodbye without any words. He headed off with the blackshirted men, never to be seen again. He left his wife and kids behind, to fend for themselves. The wife she tried as best she could, but never could recover; she dressed in black and never did take up with a lover. Each day when the sun made a hole in the sky, she'd rise and walk to the mountains high. She'd sit on the ridge and wait for a sign of Guido's coming home. She'd wait all day and into the night but Guido never once came in sight.

"The news came one day that soldiers approached the land. They came from the sea, they came from the sky and moved along the coast. Guido's wife brought her children to the mountain side and headed for the top. But as they reached the waiting ridge, the bombs began to drop. They fell like dead birds from out of the sky and made huge holes, killing a great many. They destroyed the work that Guido had done: his trulli, his country and his family. After much suffering, the war came to a close and the peasants soon disbanded. Some were buried, some stayed on in Rome, and some, like Guido made their way back home. They say that it is the soldier's fortune, to live and die by day; for fancy words he trades his life and kills because he's told. It is a story that never changes no matter how events unfold.

"Now this my friend, is the end of the story that I've hailed you to hear; but there is one more thing that you need to know and that's my real name. You see these days they call me Pazzo; but my name is really Guido. I wear this shirt of red, to remind you of the blood that I have taken and the blood that I have lost. Now take this story back home with you and remember what it cost."

For a while there I tell you I thought I wasa never goan comea back home. For those short days I was inna Italia, my mind was so busy to remember the old daze that was like La Merica was becomin a foreign country again. That's what happens to you even when you take a small vacation. Your home changes insidea you mine; it looks different, feels different. So when I was inna the plane comin home I was thinking like was the first time I come to La Merica onna boat back in the 20s. With all these thoughts in my head I fall asleep and of course "I pensieri di letto, guidano il sogno." That's summatin my nonna use to say; "The thoughts you take to bed at night, guide you dreams." Now I was stretchin my legs out under the seat inna front of me and soon I wasa snoozin away.

When the plane land in New York, the first thing I do is buy a newspaper to see if I could fine out what was ahappen when I was gone. The biga headline read: "Nuclear Leak Fogs Chicago." When I get to Chicago, I'mma stand in the airport waiting for my bags and readin the paper. The story says wasa big leak from a power plant that enter the air joosta two days before. Was a highly dangerous leak, but there seemed to be no visible effects. So I didn't think too much about it until I was waitin for my kids to come pick me up. I wait for one hour, for two, then I say to myself I know I told my kids when I'mma come home. Why they no there?

I wait another hour then I'm gettina mad. So I call up my boy's house. When he answer the phone I say, "Eh cafone, whatta you doin home? I'mma wait here for t'ree 'ours. What wrong for you? I'mma tired. He say, "Who is this, please?" I say, "Listen you stupido, I'mma you father and more than that I'mma you mad father. Why you doan come and get me from the airaport?" He say, "You must have the wrong number," and he hang upa the phone.

Now I'm thinkin is a big joke, no. My boy he joosta havein some fun with me. So I call back. But the same thing she happen. Now I'ma gettin really mad. So I jump inna taxi and go right to his house. I knock onna door and he open it up. His face was blank an he ask me what I want. I say, "Eh, doan play with me; I'mma you father an you better explain why you doan meet me at the airaport." He slama the door in my face. Now I'm gettin really mad, so I pound onna door like a craze man. But he joosta look outta window and shake his fist at me. I start to kick onna door. Well in a few minutes, the police come. They make my boy open the door and t'ree times he tell him he doan know me. I take out my passaport and show the cops that I'm tellin the truth, but it doan makea difference; they haul me away. I tell them to take me to my home and when they do I go nex' door to ask my cousin Vincenzo what's goin on with my boy. An he do the same thing to me. He call the police and now I'm inna some big trouble. They tell me I must be lost or craze.

They take me to the station and let me make some phone calls, but everyone I call doesn't know me. I tell the cops must be something to do with that nukea plant leak, must erase everbuddy's a memory. But they look at me like I'm even amore craze. Then I think maybe the only people who know me enny more are my paesani back in Italia. So I tella the police, "Take me back to the airport."

Now that wasa crazy dream, no? But in many ways it really was a prophecy of what woudla happen when I get back.

Whenever you comea back froma vacash is like you need a nudder joosta for to getta back inna swing ofa the things, eh? Well wasa likea that for me when I getta back froma Italia. My keeds wasa all there atta airaport to pick me up. Wasa nice to see them, but I wasa so tire from a the longa flight, that I wasa not too good to be around.

Wasa funny thing that happen I gotta tell you about. When I see my kids the first thing I say to them was in Italian; then the second thing I say to them was in Italian; wasa like I wasn't gonna speak English no matter what. When my Gianni boy ask me why I'ma speakin joosta Italiano, I snap back at him like he was amy old Irish work boss. Right inna airaport I was yelling at him in Italian. Well my boy he learn someatin that I doan do, and that is to leave a craze man alone. I wasa speakin nothin but Italian all the way home.

When I fine out they had a bigga festa waiting for me I get a little jumpy and tell them I joosta wanna go home. But they doan lissen a me. They take me over to Franco's house and his wife makea big turkey dinner, like wasa Thanksagivin day or somethin. Well they have alla kids there and everyone was ready for a biga party. But I wasn't inna mood. I was joosta talkin in Italiano, was like I wasa possess or someatin.

My lil grandodder wasa sittin across froma me atta table and she say, "Who is this guy? He's not my Grandpa." Then she go on an on about how I wasa different than her grandpa an maybe somebuddy kidnap they real grandpa inna Italia and some imposter take his place; all the kids was gettin afraid of me. It wasa make me all mixup that I didn't a know what to do. Was really like I wasa different man. I didn't eat, I didn't talka no more; I was joosta a crabby man. My boys take me home and I don't talk.

I tell you I was likea that for a longa time. Joosta speakin Italian, even to the mailman who isa Chinese. One mornin I was inna grocer store shoppin and I take a whole loaf of merican bread and squish all togedder so was like one piece. The bagaboy look at me like I wasa craze. He yell at me to stop it and I leavea the cart right inna middle of the aisle and walk out the store screamin in Italian.

I doan know what it was that get into me, but I wasa feelin likea stranger in my home. I wasa all confuse for days. I doan answer my phone and I don't watch the televish. All I eat was a bread from the Italian store and coffee. Then someatin happen that change me from that mood.

It wasa morning and I was slicin my bread. I was thinking today maybe I'll make somea toast. So I try to put the bread inna toaster, and no matter how I slice it, it doan fit in. I was gettin real mad so I take a slice and smush it in. Pretty soon the toasta machine start to smoke and the crust of the bread catch afire. I get so mad that I pour my coffee onna top to put out the flames. Then I reach in to pull out the toast and I getta shock. It make me so mad I pull the machine out of the wall and throw it down. It slid across the floor and land in front ofa the sink.

I was standin there lookin at this stupid machine and for some reason it make me laugh and I laugh for a longa time. There was someatin so funny about that fancy toaster lyin on the floor inna pool of coffee and bread crumbs that make me realize joosta what's abeen wrong with me.

All these years I been tryin to fit into this land of La Merica and I livea pretty good, but I was a not made to fit into the way this country was a design. I'mma like that bread and when I get stuck I get all hot and mad and burn up, and no matter how I try I wasa not made for this place. My trip back to Italia make me see that, ma come ci fa? What you goan do?